BUILDING

OUTDOOR

Kitchens

for Every Budget

CRE**A**TIVE
HOMEOWNER®

BUILDING
OUTDOOR
Kitchens
for Every Budget

Steve Cory
and
Diane Slavik

CREATIVE HOMEOWNER®

BUILDING OUTDOOR KITCHENS FOR EVERY BUDGET

AUTHORS	Steve Cory, Diane Slavik
SUPERVISING EDITOR	Timothy O. Bakke, Sr.
DESIGN AND LAYOUT	David Geer
PRODUCTION COORDINATOR	Robyn Kamholtz
PROOFREADER	Alison Daurio
INDEXER	Schroeder Indexing Services
DIGITAL IMAGING SPECIALISTS	Fred Becker, Segundo Gutierrez

Manufactured in China

Current Printing (last digit)
10 9 8 7 6 5 4 3 2 1

Building Outdoor Kitchens for Every Budget
Library of Congress Control Number: 2011926544
ISBN-10: 1-58011-537-3
ISBN-13: 978-1-58011-537-7

CREATIVE HOMEOWNER®
www.creativehomeowner.com

Creative Homeowner books are
distributed by
Fox Chapel Publishing
1970 Broad Street
East Petersburg, PA 17520
www.FoxChapelPublishing.com

Safety

Although the methods in this book have been reviewed for safety, it is not possible to overstate the importance of using the safest methods you can. What follows are reminders—some do's and don'ts of work safety—to use along with your common sense.

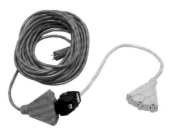

- Always use caution, care, and good judgment when following the procedures described in this book.
- Always be sure that the electrical setup is safe, that no circuit is overloaded, and that all power tools and outlets are properly grounded. Do not use power tools in wet locations.
- Always read container labels on paints, solvents, and other products; provide ventilation; and observe all other warnings.
- Always read the manufacturer's instructions for using a tool, especially the warnings.
- Use hold-downs and push sticks whenever possible when working on a table saw. Avoid working short pieces if you can.
- Always remove the key from any drill chuck (portable or press) before starting the drill.
- Always pay deliberate attention to how a tool works so that you can avoid being injured.
- Always know the limitations of your tools. Do not try to force them to do what they were not designed to do.
- Always make sure that any adjustment is locked before proceeding. For example, always check the rip fence on a table saw or the bevel adjustment on a portable saw before starting to work.
- Always clamp small pieces to a bench or other work surface when using a power tool.
- Always wear the appropriate rubber gloves or work gloves when handling chemicals, moving or stacking lumber, working with concrete, or doing heavy construction.
- Always wear a disposable face mask when you create dust by sawing or sanding. Use a special filtering respirator when working with toxic substances and solvents.
- Always wear eye protection, especially when using power tools or striking metal on metal or concrete; a chip can fly off, for example, when chiseling concrete.
- Never work while wearing loose clothing, open cuffs, or jewelry; tie back long hair.

- Always be aware that there is seldom enough time for your body's reflexes to save you from injury from a power tool in a dangerous situation; everything happens too fast. Be alert!
- Always keep your hands away from the business ends of blades, cutters, and bits.
- Always hold a circular saw firmly, usually with both hands.
- Always use a drill with an auxiliary handle to control the torque when using large-size bits.
- Always check your local building codes when planning new construction. The codes are intended to protect public safety and should be observed to the letter.
- Never work with power tools when you are tired or when under the influence of alcohol or drugs.
- Never cut tiny pieces of wood or pipe using a power saw. When you need a small piece, saw it from a securely clamped longer piece.
- Never change a saw blade or a drill or router bit unless the power cord is unplugged. Do not depend on the switch being off. You might accidentally hit it.
- Never work in insufficient lighting.
- Never work with dull tools. Have them sharpened, or learn how to sharpen them yourself.
- Never use a power tool on a workpiece—large or small—that is not firmly supported.
- Never saw a workpiece that spans a large distance between horses without close support on each side of the cut; the piece can bend, closing on and jamming the blade, causing saw kickback.
- When sawing, never support a workpiece from underneath with your leg or other part of your body.
- Never carry sharp or pointed tools, such as utility knives, awls, or chisels, in your pocket. If you want to carry any of these tools, use a special-purpose tool belt that has leather pockets and holders.

Contents

Introduction

To quote Clemens Jellema, a world-class deck builder in the Washington, D.C., area, "Everyone wants an outdoor kitchen, but most people think they can't afford one." Well, this book will fix *that*.

Many homeowners have become intrigued with the idea of an outdoor kitchen—a place to cook and prepare food with family and friends outside the confines of the house. If you live in parts of the West or the South, chances are that you know several people who have outdoor kitchens. If you live elsewhere, you may have seen outdoor kitchens in books or heard that wealthy people near you have one.

A certain type of outdoor kitchen counter has come to be accepted as the norm in some parts of the country. It is built massively and must be supported by a thick concrete slab. The appliances—grill, side burner, refrigerator, sink, and specialty items made just for outdoor kitchens—are expensive. (Many people spend more than $6,000 for a grill alone.) A pizza oven or fireplace can cost $10,000.

All considerations taken together, the cost of an outdoor kitchen like this is typically a minimum of $25,000. Many people spend $70,000 or more.

These expensive kitchens are beautiful. If they are built correctly, with reliable appliances properly installed, they can provide service for many years. And if you have that kind of cash lying around, you may choose to hire a contractor to build one.

But what about the rest of us? Many of us would rather devote our "extra" tens of thousands of dollars to paying the mortgage or putting kids through college. Must we be content with a standalone grill and a few sticks of lawn furniture?

The answer is a resounding no. In this book we will show you how to build an outdoor counter that houses all of the appliances you want . . . *for a reasonable price*. There are many ways to do this, and we will show you how to do it yourself or hire a professional to build it for you.

BELOW You will learn how to build a great counter like this—or how to save money if you hire a pro.

OPPOSITE Building with bricks that match the house makes an outdoor kitchen counter feel as if it really belongs.

Dreaming & Planning

Your goal is to build an outdoor kitchen that is inexpensive, but that does not mean you have to start out thinking small. *Don't fail to dream.* Start by thinking of all of the things that you would like—a large-enough counter in a shape that best meets your needs, the countertop, side-of-counter surfaces, cabinets, drawers, a refrigerator, a sink, an overhead structure, and last but not least the grills and burners that you have dreamed about.

Look through this chapter for inspiration and practical solutions. Later, when you add up the numbers, you may need to scale back or leave space to add additional upgrades. Or you may be pleasantly surprised to find that you can fit most if not all of the features that you would like into your budget.

Once you have an idea what you like and can afford, check out Chapter 2 (beginning on page 48), which gets specific about saving money without sacrificing goodies. Begin with a plan that copies other kitchens you have seen. Then as you think through how you will use the space, your plan should come into focus.

Bringing It All Outdoors

Even when a backyard barbecue consists of a simple charcoal grill and a few lawn chairs on the deck or lawn, the outdoor setting creates a naturally convivial atmosphere, and the food seems to taste better and is more fun to prepare. The downside is all of the trips back and forth, the mess in the indoor kitchen, and the general lack of creature comforts.

An outdoor kitchen solves these problems, bringing outdoor cooking and dining to a new level: food preparation is easier; the cooking experience is better; and the chef and diners have comfortable places to hang out. Adding an outdoor kitchen increases the time that a family spends outdoors, and it relieves stress on the indoor kitchen (and the cook). It effectively increases the square footage of the home's living space and the value of the home.

With the ever-growing number of products on the market, there are amenities to fit every budget. If your budget is tight, plan bigger than you can afford—leaving room for future upgrades. As you plan, think of your space as an outdoor dining/living room, designed for comfort and relaxation so that everyone who uses the space—cooks and their advisors, diners, and loungers alike—will feel at home.

OPPOSITE The pergola over this kitchen keeps the area shady but still wide open to the yard.

TOP Wood cabinetry is unusual in an outdoor kitchen, but it can be durable if you use rot-resistant wood and extra-strong finishes.

LEFT Stackable block assembles quickly and has the look and durability of natural stone.

ABOVE This counter's rough stone veneer complements the smooth flagstone patio.

Cooking and Entertaining Styles

An outdoor kitchen will encourage your family to eat outside more often, making for less mess and more-relaxed meals. And for those occasions when you need to cook for a larger crowd, an outdoor kitchen will make the job easier. Even a small outdoor kitchen essentially doubles your cooking space, giving you two separate kitchen areas and separate domains for chefs. Homeowners who live in cold climates increasingly grill outdoors even when it is too cold to eat there. Cooking a big turkey dinner at Thanksgiving, for instance, is easier when you can cook the main course outside on the grill and devote the indoor kitchen to all of the side dishes.

Entertaining in the summer allows you to move the messiest aspects of the meal outdoors. If you are hosting a child's birthday party, for example, you can let the kids make their own pizzas on a table that you have brought outside for the occasion. Then they can cook (supervised, of course) their creations on a grill-top pizza stone or in a pizza oven if you have one. Even if the kids get into a food fight, your indoor kitchen will remain unscathed. You can hose off the deck or patio afterward.

To design an outdoor kitchen that works for you, it helps to think about your cooking and entertaining style. Here are a few questions to ask:

- **How much will local climate limit your use of an outdoor kitchen?** If your backyard is too hot or rainy or too cold or buggy, consider the products shown on pages 32–33 and 78, respectively, which may prolong your grilling and outdoor-dining season.

- **Do you like to cook by yourself or with others helping?** How many workstations do you normally use to prepare a meal? Do you prefer to just grill outdoors, or do you like to cook side dishes and prepare salads outside as well?

- **What is your entertaining style?** Do you prefer separate grilling and dining areas or a single grilling counter where you can quickly serve diners who watch as you grill?

- **How convenient are your indoor kitchen's sink and refrigerator to your outdoor space?** If they are nearby, adding outdoor appliances may not be worth the trouble and expense.

- **Which appliances and extras do you most desire?** Think back on family cookouts and larger gatherings in the past, and make a wish list in order of priority. Of course, you will want a grill that will cook the way you want to cook. Maybe there are other dream features that will make you happy, such as a fridge, sink, or even a stereo or TV.

OPPOSITE LEFT The separate buffet counter in this kitchen lightens traffic around the cooking counter.

OPPOSITE RIGHT Here, serious diners can sit at a table; snackers and drinkers can pull up to a bar.

ABOVE This full-service counter includes grill, side burner, refrigerator, warming drawer, sink, and kegerator.

RIGHT This U-shape counter gives the cook a perfect work triangle and shields diners from grilling smoke.

The Floor

Your outdoor kitchen counter will probably rest on or abut a patio or a deck. This book concentrates on outdoor kitchens. If you need to install a new deck, porch, or patio, see Creative Homeowner's books on those subjects. (*Ultimate Guide: Decks* and *Ultimate Guide: Walks, Patios & Walls*)

Most of the designs in this book are lightweight enough that they can rest on any surface that is relatively strong. (If you build a counter using concrete block, first pour a deep concrete footing to keep the structure from cracking and sinking.)

The floor where you cook will, of course, receive spatters and spills. That is not a problem with, say, composite or vinyl decking, which you can easily wipe clean. But other common surfaces—wood decking or a patio made of brick, stone, or concrete pavers—will not be as easy to keep clean. To solve this problem, you can seal the surface with a deck or masonry sealer. Apply several coats to keep the area relatively impermeable and easy to clean. Or lay down an outdoor rug, or do both.

A Rug Near the Grill

Grease spatters and spills can stain or damage flooring right by the grill, so consider using an outdoor rug to protect your patio or deck.

LEFT Many composites today have sumptuous wood tones yet never need staining and easily wipe clean.

ABOVE The wide joints between stone pavers on this patio provide space for sturdy crevice plants, which seem to hold it all together.

FAR LEFT Ceramic tiles with a stone appearance can be mortared onto a solid concrete slab.

LEFT Carefully cut slate tiles form a neat crazy-quilt pattern.

BELOW Concrete pavers are available in groupings that form circular patterns and can be set in sand.

Sizing and Situating the Kitchen

Two of the first design decisions you will make are the size and location of the kitchen counter. Here we show some possible outdoor kitchen arrangements designed to meet different needs.

ABOVE At the far edge of the patio, this cooking center keeps heat and fumes away from diners. It is an attractive complement to the landscaping.

RIGHT This spacious patio has room for several different use areas. The cooking center is close enough to the house to make trips in and out easy, and an entertainment counter on the other side of the patio is perfect for sipping drinks on movie night.

ABOVE Built on a concrete slab along the edge of the deck and a good distance from the indoor kitchen, this spacious kitchen has plenty of amenities to minimize the need for trips back and forth.

RIGHT This outdoor kitchen's location capitalizes on the view, for both the chef and the diners. Be sure that a new kitchen with a great view does not itself obstruct a view that you have been enjoying from inside the house.

Size

A capacious counter with lots of workspace and several cooking appliances makes sense if you think you will often host large outdoor parties. But bigger is not necessarily better. If large gatherings will be rare, a gigantic counter may make your family feel dwarfed during everyday intimate gatherings. In this case, setting out extra tables for work surfaces and dining to accommodate occasional big events may be the logical solution.

Be sure that the counter is large enough if you plan to do prep work outside rather than inside—especially if several people may be cooking together. A long, straight counter works fine for up to 6 or 8 feet. If you want more counter space than that, an L- or U-shape may work better so that you don't have to traipse all the way to one end to fetch a bowl of food or utensils. Some rules of thumb:

- At least 2 feet of counter space on each side of a grill provides room for platters of cooked and uncooked meats, a medium-size cutting board, and an additional bowl for vegetables to be cooked.
- Plan on 2 feet of space next to a side burner.
- Allow at least 16 inches on each side of a sink for a drainer and bowls.
- Think of how much space you use in your indoor kitchen, and mimic that if possible. If food preparation will be elaborate, using lots of dishes and equipment, then the more counter space you can provide, the better.

Location

When situating a grill within a counter, the challenge is to place it near the home's existing kitchen for the sake of convenience but not so near that it infringes on the house's interior. Some considerations:

- If you will install a sink, natural-gas grill, or electrical outlets or appliances, aim to place the counter where you can easily run plumbing pipes (both water supply and drain), a gas line, and electrical service. Consult with contractors.
- Think through the traffic patterns. There should be as straight a path as possible from the kitchen door to the outdoor counter without running into diners or loungers. You may be able to use a window as a food pass-through. (See photo bottom left.)
- Make sure that smoke and fumes will be carried away from the house. If the grill will be on an enclosed patio, plan to install a commercial-size range hood to remove smoke.
- Take note of prevailing winds and sunlight patterns during the times of the year when you will use the outdoor kitchen. If the proposed site is not well protected from wind or sun, either move it or plan to install an overhead shade structure or a fence or hedge to minimize wind.
- There are advantages to attaching the outdoor kitchen to a house's exterior wall: utility lines are easy to run, and it is near the kitchen and protected from weather. On the other hand, a freestanding structure away from the house allows more leeway in designing the style and shape of the counter, enhances the outdoor feel, and ensures that cooking smoke will not be a problem.
- Avoid placing a counter or overhead where it will block the view of your backyard from the deck or from inside the house.

The owners situated this kitchen so that food and supplies can be conveniently passed through a kitchen window. The counter is low enough that it does not obstruct the view from the window, and the grill's location along the side of the house allows smoke to easily escape.

Blending with the House

ABOVE This counter's stone sides do not imitate anything on the house, but they do pick up on the blue-gray color of the siding and coordinate with the base of a nearby column, making the kitchen look at home.

BELOW Brick detail work that coordinates with the home's exterior lends dignity and formality to this food-prep counter. The stone countertop is of a different color, but its rounded nosing echoes nearby pillar bases.

When deciding on how the counter will relate to the house, you may aim for

- **A kitchen and dining area that blends seamlessly with the home,** borrowing colors and shapes from the house's exterior.
- **An outdoor room that contrasts sharply with the rest of the house**, thereby creating a sort of mini-vacation spot.
- **A combination of the two,** with basic "bones" that mimic the rest of the house, plus splashes of creative differences in texture, color, and style.

Builders often recommend borrowing from architectural details of the house, especially if the outdoor kitchen will be located adjacent to the home. If your new space will have a roof, for instance, try to match the shape and material of the home's roof, or install the same siding in the outdoor kitchen as that used for the home.

If the interior of the house is visible from the outdoor kitchen, consider colors and materials that complement the visible colors in the indoor flooring, wall, or countertop surfaces.

Consider your yard's landscaping, too. The site's surrounding trees, rocks, and grasses provide a palette of natural colors that you can incorporate in your outdoor kitchen, often by using local stone or lumber.

ABOVE Gray blocks used for the grill counter are also used as accents elsewhere in the house's masonry construction.

LEFT The rugged stackable blocks and bricks used for this handsome counter form a pleasant contrast with the lighter-colored masonry and trim of the house.

BELOW Stucco painted to match the house color makes this small L-shape counter appear to be a seamless extension of the home's exterior. Inset smooth river pebbles add interesting texture and contrast.

Layouts That Work

Our first tip for saving money may be of the "duh" variety, but it is well worth careful consideration: how much kitchen will you really use, and can you be just as happy—maybe happier—with less?

If the indoor fridge is nearby, for example, you may want skip installing one outdoors and perhaps install a beverage well or drop-in cooler (which holds ice and drinks) instead. Similar consideration holds for a sink.

Things that others consider luxuries, on the other hand, like a stereo system, TV, or heat source, may be near necessities as far as you are concerned.

An **L-shape kitchen** is a more spacious design that provides two distinct areas, which makes it easier for two chefs to work together. It tends to draw a dividing line between the outdoor kitchen and the rest of the yard, neatly defining the space.

Two parallel islands is a popular configuration; the second island can double as work or eating space, while the first island is for cooking. The **U-shape,** a variation of parallel islands, will accommodate plenty of appliances and amenities.

A **basic island** built onto or next to the house is a convenient and efficient design that packs everything into one compact and attractive station. If you choose to run water, electricity, or gas lines to your outdoor kitchen, it will be simplest with this arrangement. Your house will also serve as protection from the elements from at least one direction. But you will need to avoid having the back of a gas grill against the house because heat escapes at the back. A charcoal grill that is too close can cause smoke damage, too. Most grills need plenty of room all around for ventilation.

Maybe this is all you want or need: a simple counter made of the same bricks as the house encases the grill and provides a bit of food-preparation counter on each side. You will probably need to hire a bricklayer for a project like this, but the cost should be modest.

Saving on Utility Costs

TIP

Talk with your building department or local contractors to learn about any codes that might force you to spend more money.

- If you will run electrical lines for receptacles, lights, and appliances, you may be required to install a new electrical circuit, and you may be required to hire a professional electrician.
- Plumbing can be inexpensive if you run only cold water and run the sink's drain into a French drain (or dry well), as shown on page 114. Local codes may require you to connect the drain to the house's main drain, however, which can get pricy, depending on how far the drain must run and how difficult it will be to make the connection.
- If you attach a counter to the house, you may need to submit building plans and undergo framing and other inspections. You may be able to get around this by building a counter that is separate from the house. (In many areas, a counter that is not anchored to the house does not need to be inspected. Check with the local building department to be sure about this.) You may even be able to build right next to the house as long as you do not drive screws or other fasteners into the house.

ABOVE A long, straight counter allows two or more cooks to work together side by side.

ABOVE RIGHT Two large curved counters, one for eating and one for cooking, add stylish flair.

RIGHT Where no storage is needed, the countertop can simply span across supports, making ample knee room for stools.

BELOW A shape that uses two 45-deg. angles has an open feel yet keeps things in easy reach.

Dining Tables and Eating Counters

Creating a pleasant ambiance for diners in your outdoor space is similar to decorating the family room: it is a naturally more-casual area, a place to kick back and relax that allows more-creative latitude when adding personal touches, which can be fun. Whimsical art, colorful furniture, plants, or other decorations can cheerfully tie it all together. A few practical considerations follow:

- Plan a dining location that is out of the main traffic path and clear of smoke from the grill.
- If you have a pleasant view, orient the diners so that they can enjoy it. The vista does not have to be anything spectacular—a table that overlooks a few raised beds, the canopy of a nearby tree, or a trellis covered by a climbing vine or colorful plants will help everyone feel more relaxed.
- Consider a location that is entirely separate from the cooking area. You may choose to place the grill on a patio and the dining furniture on a deck, for example. The main thing is to define separate areas and to plan for traffic paths between them.
- Use several kinds of lighting fixtures and intensities for pleasant evening ambiance.
- Plan for protection from the elements to maximize the usability of the space by using overhead structures, curtains, and walls.

LEFT Here is a simple and inexpensive setup: this round table is perfect for a small urban space. You can always add another chair or two to the periphery.

ABOVE This kitchen has a freestanding grill with a long counter that doubles as a food-preparation area and dining table, situating diners so that they can talk to the chef and enjoy the view.

LEFT A built-in bench is more inviting when you add cushions. To avoid the expense of custom-made cushions, buy off-the-shelf ones before building the bench to make sure that they fit.

ABOVE This comfortable "living room" space doubles as an eating area for buffet-style dining.

LEFT Bolted to framing inside the counter, these stools swivel and can be tucked out of the way when not needed.

BELOW This stunning rustic picnic table is made of massive wood slabs. The chunky stools are simply blocks of wood. A picnic table is a good fit for an outdoor kitchen. The long bench turns a corner to clearly delineate the outdoor room.

Backsplashes

The word "backsplash" may refer to a short (perhaps 4-inch-tall) vertical piece at the back of a countertop, or it may refer to large wall section covered by easily cleanable material. An outdoor counter does not necessarily require a backsplash, but you may choose to add one because it helps define the space and can keep bowls and plates from slipping off the back of a freestanding counter.

Most grills have lids that catch all grease spatters when they are closed—and many spatters while they are open. In the flurry of food preparation, however, there will be some "friendly fire," and a backsplash can help contain it and make the area easier to keep clean.

If the outdoor kitchen is against a house wall, a backsplash will make cleaning easier and can add color and style to your design. A backsplash can also protect siding from bucking or warping due to high heat. You can use any nonflammable material for a backsplash. Stone and ceramic tiles are by far the most popular options, offering myriad design options. Brick and faux stone can also work, as long as you keep them well sealed.

If you install tiles in a sheltered place, you can attach them using mastic and standard grout. If they will be exposed to the weather, use professional-grade mortar and epoxy grout, and regularly apply grout sealer.

TOP LEFT This backsplash picks up the counter's natural brick and adds contrasting stone tilework.

LEFT Stacked bricks that travel up from the counter to the backsplash give this kitchen a monolithic, unified appearance.

ABOVE Tiles in the backsplash and along the counter edge spice up the design of this spacious kitchen.

OPPOSITE Mosaic tiles add an artist's touch to this one-of-a-kind kitchen, while the counter siding, which blends with the house, helps tie it all together.

Inside a Porch

Most of the outdoor kitchens we show in this book are open-air types. But a kitchen inside a porch (a patio or deck with a solid roof, rather than just a pergola) is also possible. Such a "semi-outdoor kitchen" has definite advantages: you can use it on rainy days and for a greater part of the year, and it may be so near to the kitchen that you will not need a sink, refrigerator, side burner, or much storage space. Be sure to heed the warnings in the sidebar "Fire Safety," right.

Fire Safety

If your outdoor space is totally enclosed, almost as if it were a room in the house, it is unsafe and probably illegal to grill because of fire and carbon monoxide hazards. If the porch has a roof but open walls, check fire codes in your area to be sure your type of grill is permitted. In dense cities, fire codes often prohibit grilling above ground level, especially for charcoal grills.

If local ordinances permit grilling on your porch, consider whether you need a range hood. If you will situate the grill against a wall of the house, you may need a range hood and backsplash to protect the house and provide a safe escape route for smoke and heat. House siding—vinyl siding in particular—exposed to high temperatures can buckle, warp, or become discolored. The same goes for the ceiling area above the grill.

If your home's exterior is made of wood or other combustible materials, the International Fire Code requires all grills, both gas and charcoal, to be at least 10 feet away from the house (though if you have an automatic sprinkler system, there may be an exception).

Read and follow manufacturer literature for your grilling equipment. With a propane grill, for example, it is a good idea to check that the tank and hose are properly connected and not leaking.

Other safety recommendations from the International Code Council (ICC) include the following:

- Place the grill away from wooden deck railings and out from under eaves and overhanging branches.
- Periodically remove grease or fat buildup.
- Do not leave a hot grill unattended.
- Store a fire extinguisher nearby.

LEFT Though modest looking, this vent hood has a powerful fan to suck out smoke.

OPPOSITE This grill has plenty of open space around it, so the owners need the vent hood only when things get really smoky.

Walls and Curtains

Outdoor walls may, indeed, not be walls at all but rather fences or other structures designed to provide privacy. A trellis covered in climbing plants or even a row of bushes or short trees may provide the privacy and wind protection you desire. If you have a nearby neighbor, a trellis with small openings may be a good compromise, providing privacy without the unfriendly feeling of a solid fence.

Wood lattice and weatherproof fabric panels provide privacy and protection from the elements. If your outdoor space has a structure, like a pergola, you can add style and color by hanging curtains or blinds. It also helps define the dining area as separate from the cooking area. If you do not have a structure, consider draping fabric over a garden trellis or whatever is available. Adding an outdoor rug and a few pillows makes the outdoor space feel cozy and inviting.

Standard low-budget lattice panels, made of thin pieces of rough-cut wood crisscrossed at a 45-degree angle, tend to look tacky and cheap (in the worst sense of the word) when used in areas other than their intended purpose: hiding the structural area below a deck or porch. It may be worth the extra cost to buy more-expensive panels or to make the trellis yourself. If you do not object to a trellis with wide spaces, you may choose to use 1×2s. For a lighter look, perhaps use a table saw to rip-cut pieces of ⁵⁄₄ decking (which is 1 inch thick), and fasten the thinner pieces in an ornamental design.

A pergola provides overhead shade and the option to hang curtains, blinds, lights, or decorations as desired. Here, a set of bamboo blinds, pulled down, adds an appealing wall of privacy and sun protection for the adjoining "room."

ABOVE Colorful fabric artfully draped over clotheslines in this urban courtyard frugally supplies sun protection while imparting a festive party mood.

RIGHT TOP Stained to match the home's cedar shingles, this privacy wall extends the warmth of wood tones to the patio; the owners use the counter as a buffet table for casual entertaining.

RIGHT BOTTOM Curtains can provide a privacy, shade, and a splash of style, but the cook may need to tie back the one in the cooking area when the grill is hot.

BELOW This wall-size trellis, created using custom-made lattice fashioned in a square pattern, brightens up a neutral seating area with climbing greenery and dappled sunlight.

Over Your Head

Protection from the elements makes an outdoor kitchen more pleasant and longer lasting. A pergola, an arbor, an awning, or a simple overhang from your home's roof each provides shade and protection from the elements. The canopy of a big tree or a few judiciously placed patio umbrellas protect you from the sun. If you add lights and a heat source for cold nights, you will transform your outdoor space into a comfortable and charming evening hangout, perfect for relaxed entertaining.

When choosing overhead elements, consider your home's architecture, landscape, and sightlines. You should not obstruct a valued view from inside the house with an overhead structure, but try to capitalize on a pleasant view from within the structure itself.

You may want to use umbrellas to add color. A range of sizes is available. Even if your table has a hole in the center, choose an umbrella with a heavy metal stand; the weight adds stability, which helps when the wind kicks up. A tilting feature is worth the extra cost because it enhances your ability to keep diners comfortable. Look for an umbrella that is easy to adjust and retract.

Awnings can be a major investment, especially if you choose a motorized retractable version. Temporary fabric shade options include pop-up canopies available at home centers. New products are always emerging; check online sources. Making your own temporary awning with fabric and poles possibly anchored by tent stakes can be fun for occasional entertaining.

LEFT An outdoor kitchen in a sunny setting is more comfortable when you provide overhead shade. Its canvas awning makes this kitchen space inviting. Many awnings are retractable; manually operated models are more affordable than motorized options.

TOP Sometimes just a little shade is needed. An umbrella that swivels can be angled as needed to block rays. This kitchen has some shade from an overhang, and the umbrella is a nice supplement for the chef.

ABOVE To extend the shade for this kitchen, rustic beams attached to the roof eave support top pieces made of two 2x4s fastened in an L-shape. The combination of wood, stone, and painted concrete block (on the house) is warm and playfully eclectic.

ABOVE This cedar pergola with widely spaced lattice on the sides neatly frames and brightens up the kitchen area. The pergola also makes it possible to discreetly run wiring for the lanterns at each end.

LEFT If bugs are a problem, a screened-in gazebo like this is one solution. Gazebos are very difficult to build from scratch, but a skilled homeowner can assemble a reasonably priced kit in a few days.

For the City Folk

Urban homes may not have the spacious backyards of their sub- and ex-urban counterparts, but lately city-dwellers are adding more amenities that make cooking, dining, and entertaining outdoors more inviting. A countertop island can hold a number of amenities. If space is tight, it may work best to place a portable grill on the island's countertop when you need it and stow it underneath when not in use. That way, the countertop can serve a number of purposes—a buffet surface, a place to show off plants, perhaps a place for children to create messy concoctions.

In the city, it is more important to minimize the effects of noise, smoke, and light from or on neighbors, and if you are going to spend more time outdoors, you may need to add privacy features like fences, trellises, or hedges.

Fire prevention and protection from falling are particular concerns for city rooftop decks, so check codes and regulations for grill-placement recommendations. There should be a solid railing all around so that children and tippling adults cannot fall off the roof. The local fire department may offer a checklist of guidelines that will keep your home and your neighbors' homes safe.

Local codes can be strict: in some cities, rooftop grilling is not permitted. You will need to be sure that the roof structure is strong enough for the kitchen, and you must install it in a way that will not damage the roof. Small, lightweight units are the norm because you can easily move them when the roof needs repairing.

ABOVE This compact open U-shape, which hugs the adjoining wall and part of the roof space, takes the place of a railing and frees up territory for dining and other activities.

LEFT A ledge behind the grill doubles as a buffet area for drinks and food and takes up almost no additional patio space. The high wood fence at the edge of the property creates privacy.

OPPOSITE A privacy wall is often essential for comfort in an urban outdoor kitchen. This custom-made horizontally oriented wall is a classy alternative to traditional lattice.

The Grill

Food seems to taste better when it is cooked outside: it tends to be hotter right off the grill, and the splash of meat juices on neighboring vegetables improves the flavor of the whole meal. The grill is the centerpiece of an outdoor kitchen, and experts advise splurging to the extent that your budget permits.

The grill tends to be the focal point of an outdoor kitchen. If you plan to build it into a countertop, you will want a grill that will last because replacing it can be a major project. Experts recommend using a minimum of Type 304 stainless steel ("Buying Considerations," page 38) or a powder-coated grill with a solid warranty.

Gas or Charcoal? The debate continues to rage in the backyards of outdoor chefs. Gas grills have the advantage of speed and convenience, making it easy to prepare a fast meal after a long day at work. Cooking with charcoal imparts a smokiness that many people consider a necessary part of the barbecue experience. (At barbecue contests, you will usually see far more charcoal than gas grills.) You can achieve great results using an inexpensive round or rectangular charcoal grill, but a built-in grill may be easier to keep clean. Make sure you can easily clean out the ashes. Some grills are sold with both gas and charcoal options, and some kitchens incorporate both types.

This gas grill includes "flavorizer" bars beneath the grate, which enhance flavor and make gas-grilled food taste more like charcoal-grilled fare.

What to Look for in a Gas Grill

You want burners rated at 12,000 Btu or more; an 8,000-Btu burner may not heat as fast as you like.

Avoid plain steel grates. They crack and develop pits, which make food stick. Stainless steel is better but will eventually lose its non-stick qualities. Porcelain-coated (or enameled) steel grates perform well but can crack if you use metal utensils. Many chefs prefer plain cast iron, which never cracks but requires regular cleaning and oiling. The best homeowner choice is probably porcelain-coated cast iron, which resists cracking and is easy to keep clean.

Kamado Grills

Tracing its origins to ancient Japanese earthenware ovens and stoves, the kamado-type cooker today is marketed as a multifunctional outdoor grill. People who own a kamado grill often wax rhapsodic when describing it because it can cook like a stovetop, oven, or grill. A number of companies make kamados, and prices vary widely. Inexpensive metal types are not as effective as ceramic models. With this kind of grill, you use a miserly amount of chunk-type charcoal. When closed, the grill can quickly heat up to 650 degrees F and hotter, or you can turn the controls for slow cooking. If you buy a unit that includes both a heat disperser and a pizza stone, the kamado grill can function much like a pizza oven for cooking homemade bread or crunchy-crust pizza.

These grills are round, so building around them calls for a circular cutout. See pages 180–83 for tips on installing one.

ABOVE Many grills include extensive shelving for keeping cooked food warm while you grill the second course. This is especially valuable for vegetables.

Evo Grill

The Evo is a gas-fired flattop stainless-steel grill with a controllable flame that is enclosed beneath the cooking surface, so food does not get charred as it would with direct fire. It has the versatility of a griddle, and many people believe that it is a healthier alternative. It has two temperature zones, which can vary from 250 to 700 degrees F. Its circular spill-collection system around the periphery funnels drippings into a drawer that can be cleaned in the dishwasher. It can use propane or natural gas as its fuel.

Most drop-in countertop grills are stainless steel, but black is also a popular choice. If you have several stainless accessories, it can break up the monotony.

A Grill Cover is a Good Investment

TIP

Your grill may come with a cover, but if not, a winter cover will protect the finish and prolong the life of the grill. This custom-made cover also covers the entire cooking counter.

Buying Considerations

■ It is often best to buy a grill that is a little better than you think you need—but not a whole lot better.

■ Shop carefully. Some grills with high-profile brand names actually deliver on features, grilling power, and durability. But then again, other high-cost and well-known grills may be disappointing. Any time consulting with homeowners, builders, and grill dealers will be well spent because it can steer you away from bad deals. Some really well-made grills are surprisingly inexpensive. The grill dealers mentioned in the "Resource Guide" at the back of the book all have good records.

■ How big is big enough? If you usually cook only for your family, a modest 26-inch-wide grill with two burners may be just fine. If you have plans for occasional parties and large events, it may be worth spending more for a 36- or even a 48-inch-wide model with four, six, or more burners.

■ How hot is hot enough? A grill's Btu number will tell you how much the whole unit will generate but will not tell you how hot each burner gets. A good rule of thumb: try to get 100 Btu per square inch. A 500-square-inch grill, for instance, should be rated at 50,000 Btu from the main burners.

■ The stainless steel used for the body should be 20 gauge or better. Thinner gauges (say, 26 gauge) are easily dented. There are many types of stainless steel, but the two most common options are Type 201 or 202, which may corrode and rust after some years, and Type 304 (also called A2 stainless), which is more likely to stay great-looking for decades. The manufacturer's literature may not tell you the type of stainless used; you may need to go online and look at the specs or consult with a salesperson.

ABOVE An enormous grill—48 in. or wider—may seem an extravagance, but it allows you to cook everything at once, without crowding.

LEFT A grill that includes ample storage space simplifies the task of building a counter, and built-in storage space like this will be easier to keep clean.

Pizza Ovens

Aficionados will tell you that the ultimate way to cook pizza is in an outdoor wood-burning pizza oven that reaches very high temperatures. These ovens are also great for baking artisan breads with a crunchy crust.

A true Italian-style pizza oven's chamber is made of Italian clay or refractory concrete, with firebricks on the floor. These masonry components provide the right humidity to produce the crustiness of Old World breads. A stone or concrete pizza oven insert has a domed roof, which radiates intense heat evenly so that the pizza or bread loaf cooks the same throughout, with no burned spots.

Cooking with a wood-burning oven is not easy. You first build the fire, then tend it until the oven reaches the desired temperature (as high as 750 degrees F). This can take ½–2 hours. Once you have attained the heat level, you push the fire to the side and slide in the pizza. It will cook in a couple of minutes and emerge with a crispy crust and distinctive smoky flavor. If you have a crowd to feed, you can cook a dozen pizzas in rapid succession.

Pizza ovens are often as good looking as they are good cooking. The oven itself is supported by a structure that raises it to chest height, with a stucco surround and a roof overhead containing a chimney, which you should keep well away from the house. Stucco and roofed ovens (page 184) look like charming little houses for your baked goods, but metal models also have appeal. (See pages 102–03 for a metal pizza oven.)

Cheaper Alternatives

Before you spring for an actual pizza oven, consider some other options:

- Although it is not in the same class as a pizza baked in a genuine wood-fired oven, many people enjoy grilled pizza. With practice, you can cook pizza on a standard charcoal grill. (Spread a bit of olive oil on one side of the dough; cook it on the grill; turn it over; spread toppings on the cooked side; then cook the uncooked side.) The result does not have the same genuine texture, but it is crunchy and has a pleasant smoky flavor.

- Other outdoor-cooking enthusiasts bake pizzas in a kamado grill. If you use a pizza stone and get the temperature up to 650 degrees F or so (which happens much more quickly than in a pizza oven), you can achieve much of the same crunchiness and texture, though the smokiness may not be quite the same.

- Some companies sell all of the parts and provide instructions for building a real pizza oven set on a stand with space for firewood below, and with a weatherproof roof—for a total price of less than $3,000. They are designed to be do-it-yourself friendly, so you can build one as long as you have basic handyman skills. On page 185 we show building one of the best of these options.

Churrasco

A charcoal-fired churrasco grills meat rotisserie style. It is different from a standard rotisserie because the heat radiates from the walls, which is said to seal in juices for tender, juicy results. This is a somewhat expensive option (though reasonably priced kits are available), but if you have been to a Brazilian churrasco restaurant, you may very well consider it worth the price. Pages 188–89 show installing a churrasco from a kit.

A pizza oven opens up culinary vistas and can give your backyard a sophisticated Tuscan ambiance.

Fire Pits and Fireplaces

Fire Pits

An open fire draws people together and makes for a campfire experience. Traditional wood-burning fire pits are perfect for roasting hot dogs or marshmallows. (Although many kids these days do not like marshmallows, s'mores still seem to be universally adored.) Often fire pits are used as a second gathering spot away from the main grill, with seating arranged in a circle around the fire.

An in-ground fire pit is simplicity itself: dig a hole in a safe location, and line it with bricks or stones. After a few wood campfires, you will need to dig out the ashes. Or purchase a lightweight metal fire pit, which you can easily move as you see fit. Some units have a wide rim that can hold small plates. Quick-firing gas options are also available. You will need to run an underground gas line to it. These come in a variety of styles and materials, from metal to masonry. The fire itself may include ceramic stones or colorful fire glass or fire beads, which add sparkle to the flames. These units are not practical for cooking, but they are beautiful to look at and provide warmth with a unique contemplative style.

Fireplaces

A fireplace will make an outdoor room feel like a comfortable living room and will lure people outside. A traditional masonry fireplace is probably out of the price range for a person looking to economize: it must rest on a massive reinforced-concrete footing and be built by an experienced mason, which would probably run you $8,000 or more.

But there are other options. A lightweight masonry fireplace in kit form can be assembled quickly and then covered with stucco or veneer stones, much the same as the churrasco project shown on pages 188–89. The fireplace is light enough to rest on a firm patio or a deck with beefed-up framing, and the total cost is less than $2,000.

Another option is a metal fireplace insert. This may cost a bit less for the fireplace itself, but you will need to build framing around it and sheathe the framing with cement backer board covered with stucco or stone veneer.

A wood-burning fireplace needs a chimney, which must extend higher than nearby structures and which drives up the price. A gas-burning unit often does not need an elaborate chimney.

The Gel-Fuel Option

A gel-fuel fireplace costs about $400 and can be placed almost anywhere. The flames produced by the gel have variations that appear more natural-looking than those of most gas units.

OPPOSITE An open-hearth fireplace becomes the focal point of many patios, creating a natural gathering place for family and friends.

ABOVE This gas-fueled fire pit shoots flames through lava-stone gravel. It can be turned on, up, down, and off remotely.

RIGHT An old-fashioned, open wood-burning fireplace like this is easy to build using flat stones and mortar.

Comforts of Home

Furnishings and textiles are often the finishing touches for an outdoor kitchen, and this is where splashes of color really enliven the space. More and more weather-resistant materials have come on the market in recent years, but check the fine print on products before you buy to make sure. Accessories like an outdoor rug, a colorful shade umbrella, chair cushions, and a coat of paint on salvaged wood pieces can work together to create a space that is uniquely yours.

RIGHT Side tables like this ensure that guests have plenty of places to set dishes and drinks and make the outdoor space seem more like a living room.

BELOW This wicker chest, which doubles as a table or sideboard surface, stores furniture cushions when they are not needed.

ABOVE This set of soft, comfortable chairs, which rock, encourage guests to linger on the patio.

RIGHT A comfortable hammock like this freestanding unit is just the place for a short snooze or some quality time with a book.

BELOW This retro-style chaise longue is just the place to flop after a busy day.

Lighting the Night

There is something magical about soft night lighting outdoors; an outdoor room has a romantic appeal when gently illuminated. Too much light will dampen the effect and possibly annoy neighbors, so try low-wattage options first and gradually increase the light level if you need to. The best lighting is subtle and natural looking.

You can put low-voltage landscape lights (usually used for highlighting yard features and lighting outdoor traffic paths) to good use in an outdoor kitchen. They come in a package that includes a string of connected lights and a power pack that plugs into a regular outlet but steps down the electricity from 110 volts to 12 volts. Path lights have metal stakes that you pound into the ground; you can also buy deck lights made to be mounted on deck posts. Higher-quality low-voltage fixtures will cost more but will last longer and are better for withstanding the elements.

Solar lights have no wiring needs; they just need to be exposed to bright light during the day. Then they automatically come on at night (with most models, there is no way to turn them off). The level of illumination varies depending how much solar energy they absorb and how good the battery is. You can buy solar path lights, deck lights, and security lights, and they are usually inexpensive.

If you require brighter lighting, you may need to run cable and install standard-voltage lights. You can control these lights using switches, photocells that turn them on at night, or both.

For task lighting, consider clamp-on barbecue lights. Similar to reading lights with goosenecks, barbecue lights grab onto a grill. Also consider wall-mounted low-voltage lights. You have several festive and fanciful options, too: rope lights that are artfully strung add sparkle; twist rope lights can be wrapped around a pole or tree; and candlelit lanterns have their own special appeal.

OPPOSITE Various light sources at a variety of levels work together to brighten this outdoor space; the hanging string lights add a festive atmosphere.

ABOVE Low-voltage lights added to deck posts automatically come on when the sun begins to fade and add a soft glow to ensure that traffic paths are visible. Grill lights come in handy for nighttime cooking.

RIGHT TOP Rope lights installed along the countertop keep the food-prep area illuminated. You can hard-wire lights like these using a switch or plug.

RIGHT BOTTOM You will need standard-voltage electrical lines for this kind of lamp, which brightens the counter and surrounding area.

BELOW Gas candles like this gives off a mesmerizing glow of warmth and light to make the sitting area more inviting.

2

Getting the Most on a Tight Budget

Throughout this book you will find projects that are medium to low priced. This chapter will help you choose some modest-cost approaches to building an outdoor kitchen.

The aim is not just to be cheap but also to produce, for a reasonable price, a sound, durable kitchen that is easy to maintain. After all, if a counter has to be rebuilt or a grill replaced after a few years, you will probably lose money in the long run. The options shown in this chapter, as well as the projects and building methods shown in the rest of the book, have proven track records in a variety of climates.

The approach you choose may depend on local conditions. If you will hire the work out, you may not be able to find a contractor to build the way you want. If you are willing to build yourself, however, nearly all of the materials shown will be available, either at a home center or from online sources.

Getting More with Less

If space and budget considerations limit the size of your outdoor kitchen, you can still get a lot of mileage from a counter that contains the basics: a grilling unit, food-preparation space, and storage space for tools. As long as you have these basic ingredients, you will have plenty of cooking and entertaining options, and you will be spared some of the hassles of building a larger kitchen, like applying for permits and running utility lines.

If space and money are not that big a problem, on the other hand, you can plan for a larger kitchen and expand the size or add amenities over time as your budget permits. Experts recommend establishing zones. Most smaller outdoor kitchens will have two zones: a hot zone for cooking and a dry zone for food preparation and storage. Bigger outdoor kitchens may also have a cold zone for chilling food and beverages and a wet zone for a sink or beverage well or both.

Once you have determined which zones you would like, think about arranging them in the "work triangle" used in indoor kitchens so that access to your grill, sink, and refrigerator will be easy and unobstructed. Builders say a common mistake is to skimp on counter space. It is important to have space on each side of a grill and sink—at least 16–24 inches, which is enough for a large platter. It can be awkward when you have company and have insufficient space to serve food or put out utensils.

Think about storage and organization for your kitchen. What do you need, and where will you put it? Common items stored in outdoor kitchens include charcoal or a propane tank, cooking utensils, garbage and recycling receptacles, cleaning supplies, napkins, dishes, serving pieces, glasses, and the like. If the kitchen is small, consider hanging tools above the food-preparation area—a simple metal bar with hooks is a good solution. Open shelves or built-in niches that hold baskets make it easy to bring out supplies you need. A drawer under the countertop is always useful. The goal is to plan so as to reduce the number of times you need to walk in and out of the house.

OPPOSITE This large U-shape kitchen has lots of amenities, but the stucco and tile counter that hold it all together are not expensive. Because the outdoor kitchen is near the house, running utility lines for water, gas, and electric lights and outlets is easier.

LEFT TOP If you would like the option of cooking with both charcoal and gas, you can *plan* a counter for both and install the second unit as the budget permits. In a kitchen like this, the low shelf for the kamado grill could be used for other purposes (say, a basket of supplies) until you are ready to buy the grill.

ABOVE This honeymoon kitchen for two fits a lot of utility in a small space. Inexpensive ceramic tiles top the stucco counter, which is painted to match the house exterior, and the two-level countertop compactly provides both food-preparation and dining space.

LEFT BOTTOM This rambling patio leads to a modest-sized brick structure with upper and lower countertops, housing a grill with integrated storage doors and drawers. For a small price and size, the setup provides plenty of cooking and entertaining possibilities.

Building a Lightweight Counter Inexpensively

When you look at a typical outdoor kitchen counter, you see the facing—stone, tile, stucco, or wood—and the doors and appliances. It is usually not possible to see how it was built. What looks like a solid structure of stone may actually be built with wood, backer board, and thin stone or faux-stone veneer.

Many of the materials used for building outdoor kitchens are inexpensive, but not all are inexpensive to install. Concrete blocks, for example, do not cost a lot, but if you build a counter with block, it will be so heavy that you will need to first excavate and pour a thick reinforced-concrete footing. A handy homeowner may be able to install the block, but the job calls for practiced skill and so is usually left to professional masons. As a result, a concrete-block structure can be quite expensive.

When we talk about a "lightweight" counter, we don't mean that you can it pick it up and walk off with it; it will be solid and immovable. (The countertop itself will be quite heavy.) But counters built with studs and backer board or with PVC sheets or other lightweight materials have several advantages:

- **They can rest on an existing deck or patio,** as long as it is structurally sound. If you want to put one in the lawn, you can install a simple sand-and-gravel patio or small deck to support it.
- **Building is more homeowner friendly.** We will show you how to cut and assemble wood and metal studs and attach backer board. This calls for basic skills, not special masonry techniques.
- **Building will be quick.** You won't have to pour a footing and wait a few days for it to cure. You can simply start building.
- **If you make a mistake while working, it will be easy to fix**—which often is not the case with concrete block.

All in all, building the structure (not including the decorative facing) for an 8-foot outdoor counter will run an estimated $130 for the studs (metal or wood), backer board, and fasteners.

If you build with stackable block (pages 156–59), prices can vary widely depending on the type of block you buy. In general, you can expect to pay around $5 per block, which means that an 8-foot counter with a number of openings in the front may cost somewhere around $250.

Is It Strong Enough?

TIP

If you live in an area where all of the other outdoor counters are made of concrete block, you may hear a contractor tell you that a stud-and-backer-board counter will not be strong enough to support a heavy countertop. Rest assured, however, that many builders around the country build this way, and they do not worry about strength. A wall made using studs and backer board and covered with ½-inch-thick stucco is extremely strong and can easily support even a heavy concrete countertop, as well as the weightiest of outdoor grills, with no problem.

A Couple of Really Inexpensive Counters

Here are two simple 7-foot counters that will look familiar once you have perused the rest of this book. They were built in order to take many of the how-to photos in chapters 4 and 5, and this book provides full instructions for building them. Someone with basic how-to skills can build either counter for a low price over the course of a couple of weekends. Both use stainless-steel components—grill, door, and sink—that are moderately priced but of good quality.

We built the white stucco counter with the kamado grill and concrete countertop (below left) over the course of 5 working days. (The process was slowed substantially because we had to stop and take the photos.) In addition to the working days, the project required 7 days to allow the stucco coats to cure and 7 days to allow the concrete countertop to harden.

This counter offers the popular kamado-style grill, plus a side burner and a receptacle for appliances.

MATERIALS COSTS
2x4s and nails for framing: $35
Concrete backer board: $40
Stucco (base coat and finish coat, plus stucco lath): $50
Metal door: $220
Cedar for wood doors, shelf, and trim: $35
Concrete and colorant for countertop: $35
Kamado grill (large unit from the Saffire Company): $1,000
Side burner with piping for gas hookup: $350
Electrical receptacle, cable, box, and conduit: $30
TOTAL COST: $2,065.

We built the counter shown below right with two helpers. It took us 2½ days to build. Were it not for the time needed for photos, we could have completed it in less than 2 days. We saved a good deal of money by purchasing used granite slabs from *craigslist*.

This unit features a granite slab countertop and slate tile siding, a 36-inch gas grill of good quality, and a bar sink. We framed the counter using steel studs.

MATERIALS COSTS
Metal studs and screws: $30
Concrete backer board and screws: $40
Slate tiles (for $1.20 each at a home center): $60
Mortar and grout for slate tiles: $30
Granite slab (from *craigslist*): $150
Gas grill: $800
Bar sink with faucet and plumbing: $200
TOTAL COST: $1,130

Counter Facing

Some homeowners choose pricy stone facing for their counters, and you may feel it is worth the cost to get exactly the look you want. But you should also consider some less costly (in some cases, dirt cheap) options. (When estimating prices, we consider a typical 8-foot counter to be 3 feet tall and to have gaps for the grill and doors, for an estimated 45 square feet.)

You can apply **STUCCO** quickly, using either stucco mix or a surface-bonding agent, and color it while mixing or paint it after it has dried. It will cost less than $50 to cover a typical 8-foot-long counter. If you use stucco mix, you will need to apply a scratch coat, wait a couple of days, and then apply the top coat. If you use a surface-bonding agent, it is a one-step process. You will need only a couple of hand tools.

You can buy **FLAGSTONES** made for paving a patio at a stone yard for a low price; you will probably pay by the pound (or portion of a ton). Cutting and assembling flagstones on the side of a counter will be a bit challenging, but it does not call for special skills. You will set them in mortar, which is also an inexpensive material. A grinder, a couple of cold chisels, and a trowel or two are all of the tools you will need.

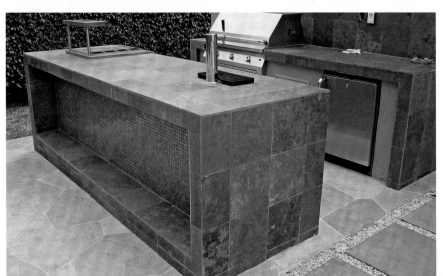

SLATE TILE produces an elegant surface with interesting variations in color. Slate prices are all over the place. Some types can be pricy, but good-looking slate often goes on sale at home centers for less than $2 a square foot, meaning that covering an 8-foot counter will cost less than $100. (Inexpensive slate may be too fragile to use on the top of a counter but will do just fine on the sides if you fully embed it in thinset mortar.)

You might want to use **CERAMIC TILE** for siding. Tiles may be large and earth-toned or small and varied in color. Of course, ceramic tile varies widely in price, but many types cost less than $2 per square foot, for a total cost of a little over $100 once you add the thinset mortar.

BRICK or **BRICK VENEER** can run from $4 a square foot and up. If you like the look of used common brick, you may be able to scavenge from a demolition site. If you want glazed or another kind of decorative brick, the price can more than double. If you have masonry skills, you may choose to build counter walls using brick instead of a stud-and-backer-board structure.

FAUX STONES and **NATURAL STONES** made for decorative siding also come in a great range of sizes and colors, as well as prices. At the low end, veneer products cost about $5 per square foot, so covering an 8-foot counter may cost about $225. But it can cost a lot more. Veneer stones are generally easier to install than flagstones or brick. If the stones you choose need to have mortared joints, expect to spend an extra day jointing.

LEFT This unusual arrangement combines stone facing with a concrete surface that seems to spill over from the (concrete) countertop.

BELOW Applying stone facing can be an opportunity to show creative flair. Here, river rocks with rounded edges are arranged in a flowing pattern.

ABOVE Composite decking can also be used as a siding material.

RIGHT This counter's siding is made of natural limestone in a range of hues.

BELOW A counter made of dry-stack blocks is finished once the stacking is done. A simple dark-red horizontal band adds just the right decorative touch.

Cabinet Options

You can make a counter by joining cabinets together, much as you would in an indoor kitchen. Of course, the materials need to be more durable and weather resistant. You will find instructions for building them yourself on pages 146–55.

Cabinets made of PVC or polymer sheets can run about $800 for an 8-foot counter, including the hinges and knobs. You will end up with a clean look that you can paint or leave alone.

Wooden cabinets vary greatly in materials price, depending on the kind of wood used. If you build with ipé, cumaru, or other Brazilian hardwoods, the cost will be steep; the same cabinets made with cedar will be less than half the cost. Wooden cabinets may employ fine cabinetry, or they can be quickly cobbled together using boards (or even sheets of wood siding) and rough doors.

Another option is to build with composite decking, which is an expensive material (though costs vary widely) but requires no maintenance once built.

Making cabinets like these yourself will require basic woodworking skills. PVC and polymer cabinets may cost more than building a basic stud-and-backer-board counter structure, but they save a good deal of money when it comes to doors, and they offer greater storage flexibility.

LEFT Made with PVC sheets, this clean-looking cabinet is topped by a variegated stone countertop.

LEFT BOTTOM The siding and doors of this counter are made of vertical hardwood strips for a seamless look.

BELOW Woodworking steps for making cabinets like these are included on pages 150–55.

OPPOSITE PVC cabinetry, shown here with beadboard panels, is attractive enough for an indoor kitchen. You may use colored sheets, or paint them when you are done with construction.

Countertops to Choose

All those gleaming granite countertops that you see in magazine photos (and in this book) may make you think that an outdoor counter is too elite a product for you. Fortunately, there are other attractive options, and even granite may not be as expensive as you think.

Granite Slab. Let's start with granite, which makes so many homeowners drool. As long as you do not require a fabulous granite slab that makes a one-of-a-kind design statement, there are ways to save money:

- **Shop.** Granite fabricating has become common in many areas, which means competition and lower prices: it may be possible to get granite cut and installed for less than $30 a square foot. Also check tile stores and home centers; some sell 8-foot-long slabs for modest prices. This varies from region to region, but it seems to be a growing trend. A retailer may even deliver to your house for a reasonable price.
- **Durability has nothing to do with how much you pay for granite. (Surprise!)** In fact, the really high-end material is often significantly more fragile, especially if it features stunning veins, which are actually almost cracks.
- **If you can't get a good price in your area, check out online sources.** A number of companies will sell and ship slabs for far less than it costs to buy locally. Shipment may take a week or more.
- **You can use a series of short pieces in an outdoor counter because the grill interrupts the flow.** After designing your counter, you may find you need only 4-foot-long and shorter pieces. (You can also discreetly splice behind the grill.) Often, granite outlets sell inexpensive leftover remnants, which may serve your purposes for far less money.
- **You can sometimes (not always) save significant money by cutting the granite yourself.** This may sound improbable, but it is really not that difficult. See pages 162–66 for instructions.

- **Consider used slabs.** Granite and quartz slabs have been around for a while, so homeowners remodeling their kitchens often will sell their old countertops. Also, check demolition companies, which also may advertise online. We bought the slabs used in the project on pages 163–65 from *craigslist* for $100. We were able to transport and cut the slab with a couple of helpers and a pickup truck.

Quartz. Because it resists staining so well and never needs sealing, quartz is probably the most practical countertop material for outdoor use. It may be more difficult to find cheaply than granite, though not impossible. Try the suggestions for granite that appear at left. You can cut quartz in the same way as you cut granite.

Concrete. The materials for a concrete countertop are stunningly low in price; an 8-foot top will likely cost less than $100. Making one yourself will be a bit of a challenge. (See pages 174–79.) But it's a satisfying creative project. Otherwise, contact a contractor who specializes in decorative concrete. There are two basic types: **(1)** An artistic concrete countertop fabricator can come up with interesting ideas and produce a top that is silky smooth, like an indoor top. **(2)** You may be able to find a local concrete contractor who pours and finishes decorative concrete driveways and patios. He or she may also do countertops on the side. The finished product may be a bit rougher, but it will probably cost a good deal less.

Tile. You can tile a countertop yourself or hire a contractor to do it for you. Tile prices vary greatly. The durability of a tiled top also varies greatly: follow our instructions (pages 168–71) closely to produce one that is durable and cleanable. You may be tempted to create your own artistic tiled top, using a crazy-quilt-like selection of small tiles or tile shards. Such a mosaic can be quite inexpensive, but there are risks: unless you are an accomplished tile artist, the results may look amateurish. In addition, laying many little tiles for a countertop that will be exposed to the outdoors can lead to a surface that cracks and comes apart in a few years.

ABOVE Beige granite, ³/₄ in. thick, can sometimes be found for a low price. The lighter color means that it will not get too hot in the sun.

RIGHT TOP Limestone, which needs to be sealed to protect against stains, makes a handsome statement for—in many locales—a reasonable price.

RIGHT CENTER Stone-look porcelain tiles are durable and will stay put if correctly installed.

BELOW Flagstones are an unusual but appealing choice because they are inexpensive and durable.

RIGHT BOTTOM Large ceramic or quarry tiles create a classy monolithic look when installed neatly and with matching grout.

Dark Countertops Can Get Hot

TIP

Gleaming dark countertops are beautiful to look at but may be too hot in the summer. Plan for shade to avoid wilting lettuce and melting ice in your drinks—or go with a lighter color.

LEFT TOP Tumbled or honed granite has a rough texture and needs to be sealed, but its natural color and imperfections have irresistible warmth.

ABOVE Bluestone slabs have a slightly grainy texture. The chipped edge contributes to the rustic rough-hewn feel that these slabs impart.

LEFT BOTTOM Polished granite is perhaps the most popular countertop material. Varieties like this, with a prominent pattern of veins, tend to cost more.

BELOW Carefully selected flagstones can form a surface that is heavily ridged but fairly level, so it is not difficult to clean.

ABOVE Hardwood is an unusual choice for an outdoor countertop, but it can work as long as it is well protected.

RIGHT This limestone countertop, with its rough-hewn edge, is expertly cut to snake around an under-mounted sink with a meandering design.

BELOW Mosaic tiles can add artistic flair; here, natural-stone tiles with solid, rounded edging are a stylish, understated choice.

Doors and Drawers

The basic ingredients for an outdoor kitchen are the grill and a food-preparation surface, but it is always nice to have storage space. One way to create storage is by incorporating ready-made weather-resistant cabinets in your design; another way is to build cavities for storage, to which you can either add doors or use as open shelving. Structures built using masonry often have small storage spaces because the concrete blocks used for building them take up so much space.

Grill manufacturers sell doors and drawers in various sizes. Shop around for the best prices; online sources may be best. If you buy stainless steel (the usual choice), get units with at least 20-gauge steel. (The lower the gauge number, the thicker the steel.) If you expect heavy use, go for 18-gauge or thicker steel. A brushed or matte finish is better than a shiny finish, which will readily show scratches, smudges, and fingerprints. Try to buy all of the components from the same company for a coordinated look.

A door will be a good deal less expensive than a drawer unit, but unless you install a slide-out unit for inside the door (for a garbage can or charcoal bin, for example), you will need to get down on your knees to get at things inside. Door cavities are fine for storing large items like a bag of charcoal, but you may want to splurge a bit for drawers to hold utensils

You can also make your own doors from exterior-grade wood, which will save a good deal of money. (See pages 142–45.) Wooden doors have an appealing handcrafted look and can be quite durable as long as you don't mind a few inevitable scratches and dings.

Make Sure Your Doors and Drawers Will Fit

Be sure to buy your doors and drawer units ahead of time, and have them on hand while you build the counter to ensure accurate sizing for openings.

LEFT Under-sink doors are usually needed so you can repair plumbing when needed.

TOP This simple box-like structure made of cement-based backer board creates shelving and makes it easier to get at items behind the door.

ABOVE Cabinet-style wood doors add warmth and make the overall design more interesting.

It Will Get Wet Inside

TIP

Builders report a nearly universal fact: no matter how well you build a counter, its inside will get at least a little wet during a heavy downpour (unless, of course, the counter is inside a covered porch). So avoid storing things that can easily rust, and provide drainage holes as needed so that the water does not sit for long.

The doors and drawer faces to the right of this grill are made of hardwood plywood protected with several coats of sealer that should be renewed yearly. The countertop's overhang helps protect them from rain.

Storage Solutions

In an indoor kitchen, slide-out accessories, often placed inside base cabinets, make it easy to reach things without having to get on your hands and knees. The same principle applies to outdoor kitchens, where a slide-out garbagecan unit can serve many purposes, from storing a bag of charcoal or birdseed to holding a cooler full of beverages on ice. As outdoor kitchens have grown in popularity, new accessories for cabinets have popped up to make the kitchen more fun to design and use— and these are generally inexpensive upgrades.

Adding open shelves, nooks, and crannies also helps keep clutter off the countertop and makes the overall design more interesting, easier to use, and more inviting.

LEFT This sink unit comes with built-in shelves and rails for hanging utensils, as well as a removable shelf in front for bar supplies.

TOP A slide-out drawer is a versatile add-on; it can be used for garbage can but can also house a cooler.

ABOVE CENTER This open shelf makes it easy to get at condiments or cleaning products.

ABOVE In this kitchen with a roof overhead, open wall shelves free up counter space and provide an opportunity to add personal touches.

This beverage center makes it easy to mix and garnish drinks. It has an insulated ice drawer, condiment holders, and a covered, heavy-duty blender.

Getting a Good Grill Value

The grill is often the most expensive item in an outdoor kitchen. Grills designed to drop into a counter can be especially costly. (See pages 36–37 for tips on choosing a high-quality grill.) But you don't have to break the bank to get good cooking equipment. Here are some tips:

- You don't always get what you pay for, so shop carefully. There is a wide range of quality among grills of the same price range. Consult with several salespeople and with grill owners before you make your decision.
- As long as you buy from a reputable company, you can be pretty sure that an inexpensive ($400–$800) grill will last about 5 seasons, while most grills that cost more than $1,000 can last 20 seasons. (Of course, this is only a general estimate.) If you have the occasional grease fire, expect the cheap grill to die sooner.
- At the very lowest end, you can build a counter around a cart (standalone) grill bought at a home center or other inexpensive outlet—or use the cart grill you already own, if it is in good shape. (See "Building around a Cart Grill," opposite, for practical tips.) These pages show several examples of cart grills used in this way.

- An inexpensive grill might suit your needs. Once it stops functioning well, you will probably be able to buy replacement parts. (You may notice the fire burning with diminishing intensity, for example, or the grill may be hard to start.) Parts are available from the manufacturer or from appliance-parts sources, which have begun to cater more to outdoor-kitchen equipment in recent years. If the shell of the grill is sound and you replace the burners and grate (and maybe the starter as well), you will essentially have a new grill. The bottom line: buying an inexpensive grill may *not* be a bad deal over the long haul. Be aware, however, that many off-brand grills may not have parts available in the future.
- If you cook a lot, it may be best to run a natural-gas line from the house to the counter (if possible and if you use natural gas in your house). Depending on the distance, a gas line does not have to cost a lot. If you will grill occasionally—say, once or twice a week for less than half the year—or do not have natural gas at your location, you can put a propane tank inside the cabinet. Be sure to install large doors so that you can easily replace the tank.

Building around a Cart Grill

Here is one way to build around a cart grill. In this case, the cabinet is made of PVC sheeting, which is fireproof, though it could melt. Attach heat-protective material to the areas where the hot part of the grill will be near the cabinet (right). In this case, the builder used a layer of cement-based backer board; you may choose to use another masonry material. You may leave the doors on the cart grill or remove them so that you can install your own doors (below). Remove the grill's wheels, and slide it into place; then build a simple frame around it (below right).

OPPOSITE A gas-and-kamado-grill combo lets you cook a fast meal on weeknights and slow smoked ribs on the weekend.

ABOVE A cart grill with integrated side tables slides up to a counter when needed.

RIGHT A counter made of stackable blocks with a stone-tile countertop attractively houses this high-end grill.

More Cooking Options

In addition to the main grill, consider some other appliances that will make it fun to cook outdoors. Some gas grills feature an infrared burner. Within a few minutes, it produces a cooking temperature in the 900-degree-F-and-higher range, which can be good if you like your steak charred on the outside but rare in the middle. A gas burner tuned to produce heat in the far infrared range focuses the heat onto a ceramic tile riddled with thousands of tiny holes, which radiates the high-temperature heat to cook food without flames or flare-ups. Fans say that the infrared heat locks juices and flavors in food. They recommend searing a thick steak for 2 or 3 minutes per side, then transferring the meat to a standard burner. Critics say that the heat is so hot, it can be tricky to get good results; some even say it is too hot for proper searing.

Small infrared grills, which resemble a toaster oven in size, are sold as portable units, but you can also build them into a counter. Some models cook with a gas infrared burner mounted over the cooking grid, others with the burner underneath. The burners generate high heat: manufacturers claim that they heat up to 1,700 degrees F and can cook pizza, fish, chicken, and steak in 4 to 8 minutes.

A deep fryer heats oil or water and can be used for steaming, boiling, or frying. It consists of a cooking insert that drops into a special gas grill in place of a grilling grate and a lift-out frying basket. Seafood lovers use the boiling feature for lobster, but it is also ideal for pasta. Adding less water, the unit is great for steaming veggies. Adding oil instead lets you deep-fry French fries, clams, or shrimp to perk up the summer menu, keeping all of the heat and mess outside.

A rotisserie rotates meat on a spit above or in front of a heat source, which may be infrared, gas flame, or charcoal. Many gas grill manufacturers offer rotisseries powered by a hidden built-in motor that rotates the spit above or in front of an infrared burner. But you can add a rotisserie unit to almost any grill. Often the grill manufacturer sells a unit to fit; it plugs into a standard receptacle. These units may require a little more attention—the main challenges being to find the right height over the heat source and to balance the weight of the meat on the spit so that the mechanism spins smoothly.

ABOVE LEFT A large motorized rotisserie slowly cooks roasts and chickens to perfection.

ABOVE A deep fryer can also be filled with water to boil lobster, crabs, or other shellfish.

LEFT Infrared burners quickly reach temperatures high enough for searing meat to seal in juices.

This pizza-oven insert has a gas infrared burner that can attain 1,700 deg. F in less than two minutes. The enclosure kit includes a chimney and masonry surfaces.

Side Burners and Warmers

If you would like to do all of your cooking outside, a side burner will give you increased menu flexibility. While the main course cooks on the grill, you can boil pasta or potatoes, steam a few vegetables, and cook a tasty sauce to pull the meal together. Side burners that come attached to grills are often too weak to boil water quickly, so it is usually better to have a separate side burner rated at 12,000 Btu or more. Look for a burner with a heavy stainless-steel grate and cover and a design that will be easy to clean. Many models have front and rear burners.

A griddle is a nice accessory to have for your grill or side burner, letting you cook bacon, eggs, and pancakes for a weekend brunch.

If you love to cook Asian food on a wok, you could simply place your wok on a side burner. However, you'll get better results if you swap out the burner grate for a special grate or burner cover with a built-in ring to stabilize a wok. That way, heat will be perfectly centered under the wok so that food in the bottom sizzles while food higher up stays warm.

Often placed at a lower level in the counter, a pot burner can handle a large stock pot, big enough to fry a turkey. These burners have a high Btu level but can also be dialed down for a small saucepan as needed. Most models feature two rings of fire on the burner—an inner ring for smaller pans and a larger outer ring for full power that operates together with the smaller ring.

Many grill manufacturers offer food warmers to match the style of the grill. Better models generate steam via a heated water bath to keep food from drying out. Warming units sometimes rest on the counter and have two or more compartments with lids, similar to restaurant buffets. Or they may be found in drawers under or next to the grill.

ABOVE LEFT This food warmer/steamer with three removable pans uses gel-type fuel canisters in the slide-out drawer below.

ABOVE CENTER With a removable ring that rests on the burner grate, this side burner will safely hold a round-bottom wok.

ABOVE RIGHT A griddle is a popular accessory that makes alfresco brunch a festive occasion.

RIGHT This gas grill with a built-in warming drawer eases the challenge of serving all of the food piping hot.

To steam veggies and boil pasta while grilling, get a double side burner like this with a high Btu rating and plenty of room for two large pots.

Sinks and Plumbing

Under-mounted sinks are practically *de rigueur* these days, especially in granite countertops in both indoor and outdoor kitchens. If you think it might be too much of a luxury outdoors, consider a self-rimming sink (with a rim that sits on top of the countertop). It requires a bit more attention during cleanup, but you can install one yourself more easily—and at a lot less cost—than an under-mounted sink. (See pages 190–91.) Twenty-gauge steel works fine because the stamping increases the strength of the sink. A standard inexpensive bar sink will perform nearly as well as an expensive model made for outdoor use.

Plumbing can be expensive, though. Consider running only cold water, which is all you need for rinsing vegetables. And instead of running the drain line into the house's main line, you may be allowed by code to run the drainpipe into a dry well (basically a hole in the ground filled with rocks, page 114).

A standard stainless-steel faucet works well; there is no need to buy a special outdoor model. You can use a T-fitting to run the water to both sides of the faucet, so both handles (or both sides of a one-handle faucet) will turn on cold water.

If you want hot water, it may be easiest to run cold water into the counter and then install a point-of-use tankless water heater inside the counter. You can plug it into a standard 120-volt electrical receptacle. (See pages 124–25 for installing a receptacle.) Another option: install an "instant hot" faucet, which also plugs into a receptacle. It produces water that is about 180 degrees F, so you can quickly brew tea and cook items like thin asparagus.

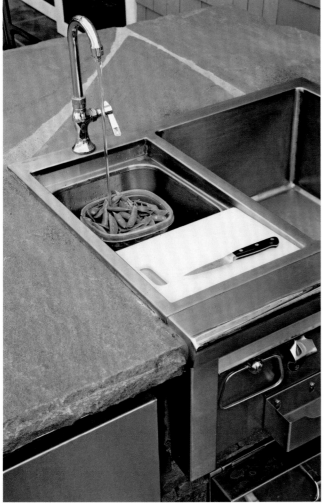

OPPOSITE As you can see here, a farmhouse, or apron, sink is surrounded by the countertop on only three sides.

TOP LEFT This self-rimming sink drops into place atop a bluestone countertop.

TOP RIGHT To install a sink under a granite top, the hole must be expertly cut and polished as shown.

LEFT Here, an apron sink is installed self-rimming style, so its lip covers the cut stone edges.

ABOVE A small sink may be all you need. For this installation, two single holes were bored for the faucet and soap dispenser.

Amenities

Here are a few of the extras that can turn a plain space into a main destination for friends and family. You can add these extras a little at a time if you are on a tight budget. After a few seasons, you will have an **UPSCALE OUTDOOR KITCHEN** (right top) that will be the envy of any neighborhood.

Television

Most **FLAT-SCREEN TVs** (right center) are easy to attach to the wall; the setup looks clean if the electrical receptacle is behind the unit. Of course, be sure to put yours in a well protected area so it will not get wet. The electronics store where you buy the TV and speakers can advise you, or you can have them install it.

Kegerator

If you are having a big party, you may want to buy a keg of beer. But after a while the beer will not be cold unless you put it in a big, ugly tub of ice. A **KEGERATOR** (right bottom) improves on the experience because it actually is a refrigerator with a keg inside, connected to a tap. It also contains a carbon dioxide tank to supply pressure. Beer kept at the right temperature and pressure stays fresh for several weeks and will taste just right when dispensed. Kegerators usually have different options for tank size, so you can fill the space with one large keg, typically one-half barrel, or two or three smaller tall kegs. Fill the kegs with beer from a local pub or brewer; buy a keg of your favorite brand at the beer or liquor store; or brew your own. Because the pressure and the temperature are adjustable, home brewers can get better results. Although a keg containing beer requires constant refrigeration, the unit should use less power than a similar-size refrigerator because you open the door only when replacing the keg or cleaning the lines. Some manufacturers specify "for indoor use only," so check that the unit you like will work for your outdoor climate.

Mosquito Abatement

According to the American Mosquito Control Association (AMCA), bug zappers and other anti-insect machines and sprays have limited effectiveness. Nipping the problem in the bud, when mosquitoes are breeding in watery places in or near your yard, is the best defense because it eliminates the bugs before they sprout wings. Once mosquitoes have reached adult stage, screens, nets, and topical lotions with DEET are what the AMCA recommends. Consider a screened-in porch or lanai or, on a smaller scale, a pop-up screened-in canopy, though you will need to keep it well away from grill flames and from pets because netting is easily damaged. New **MOSQUITO SPRAYERS** (right top) are environmentally-friendly products, and they may provide some relief. But to be really effective, your whole neighborhood would have to spray, too.

Heaters

Fire pits and fireplaces are one way to warm up your outdoor space, but patio heaters may be a more affordable and effective alternative. Available in propane or electric-powered form, heaters can take the edge off the chill within a certain range of distance. The most popular **PROPANE HEATERS** (right center) look like torchiere floor lamps that stand 7 or 8 feet tall with a 20-pound propane tank at the base. Look for a pilotless model (so you do not have to light it every time you want to use it); you can install one in a permanent location or choose one with wheels, which make it easy to move around. Tabletop heaters are also available; they tend to look like small torchiere lamps. Propane heaters radiate heat in a circle around the heat source and warm up an area ranging from 10 feet in diameter for tabletop heaters to 20 feet in diameter for floor models. A 20-pound propane tank will provide about 10 hours of heat. Propane heaters should not be used in an enclosed space.

A variety of electric heaters, which plug into regular house outlets, is available. **WALL-MOUNTED HEATERS** (right bottom) glow orange and throw heat in one direction. Tabletop and ceiling heaters, which may use halogen bulbs or infrared technology, generate heat in a more circular pattern. Check reviews before you buy. Generally, heat output from electric heaters cannot match that of propane rivals, but electric heat is good for an enclosed space.

Refrigerators and Coolers

Most outdoor chefs bring food to the grill as they are getting ready to cook and do not use their outdoor refrigerators (if they have them) to store food directly from the store. When cooks use outdoor fridges for food, they tend to use them for meat that is marinating and waiting to be cooked or side dishes prepared earlier in the indoor kitchen. Outdoor fridges are actually used most often for keeping beverages cold. Many builders recommend an ice-based beverage cooler as an attractive and energy-efficient alternative. There are a number of products that use ice and insulation to keep beverages cold. They range from a simple beverage well that rests in a table or counter cutout to a pullout ice bin or stand-alone beverage center complete with a cocktail blender. All of these options combine ice and insulation to keep beverages cold for an entire day—just fill them with ice and drinks.

If you would still like a refrigerator, however, do some research. Specialty stores sell expensive outdoor refrigerators, some specifically designed for beverages and some for wine, for $1,000 and more. But builders from around the country report that inexpensive models (around $125) last for five years or more, so you may be better off purchasing a cheaper model and replacing it a few years down the road if necessary.

LEFT An icemaker like this may seem an extravagance, but it can be cost effective if you entertain often or tend to throw large parties.

ABOVE This refrigerator, with its glass door, keeps guests and household members from unnecessarily opening and closing it to see what is inside.

TOP LEFT Most people use their outdoor refrigerator to keep drinks cold. The built-in dishwasher to the left makes cleanup easy.

TOP RIGHT The family bartender will appreciate separate cooler bins for limes, cherries, and other ingredients; of course, these bins can also hold burger condiments.

LEFT CENTER This removable, enclosed front shelf holds bartending supplies in easy reach.

ABOVE This margarita station puts the requisite heavy-duty blender at a convenient height.

LEFT BOTTOM With its adjustable temperature control, this refrigerator drawer will keep desserts frozen or just chilled.

Grilling Accessories

Personalize your grill with equipment tailored to your menu preferences. There are many specialized products that make it easier than ever to get professional results in your outdoor kitchen. These two pages feature a few popular options.

TOP Cooking fish, especially delicate fish like tilapia, sole, and flounder, on the grill can be challenging. A metal rack like this helps keep the fish intact; to minimize sticking, grease the metal before adding the fish.

ABOVE Take your burgers up a notch by stuffing them with cheese, onions, olives, mushrooms, or whatever you like. This burger basket holds it all together for you and makes flipping easy.

TOP Create your own stuffed jalapeno appetizers with this unique metal grill accessory. Stuff peppers with cheese or other ingredients; arrange them standing up in the roaster; set the roaster on the grill; and close the lid. This model comes with a corer, making it easy to remove seeds.

ABOVE Available at kitchen stores, these 1-in.-thick hand-cut slabs of salt mined in Pakistan near the Himalayas lend a hint of salty flavor to food. You can use them for cooking delicate items like thin fish and shrimp or as serving plates (popular for sushi). To clean, scrub the surface and pat it dry.

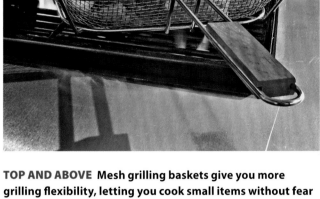

TOP AND ABOVE Mesh grilling baskets give you more grilling flexibility, letting you cook small items without fear that they will fall through the grates. Throw the basket in the dishwasher afterward for easy cleanup.

TOP Wooden planks, popular for cooking salmon, impart a smoky flavor and help food retain moisture for more-tender results. Fish slides off easily after cooking. Soak the plank for an hour before using it; then it place on the grill. This metal holder makes it easy to remove the plank from the grill. (Wear gloves!)

ABOVE Desserts are not commonly prepared on the grill, but campfire favorite s'mores have nostalgic appeal for adults and are always popular with kids. This ingenious device cooks marshmallows on a spit, which you rotate by (gloved) hand while melting chocolate atop crackers on a rack.

Doing It Yourself or Hiring a Pro

As this chapter has shown, it is possible to build an attractive and durable outdoor kitchen for a modest materials cost. But the major expense with most outdoor kitchens is labor, not materials. So perhaps the most important economic decision you will make concerns how much of the work you will hire out and how much you will do yourself.

Fortunately, an outdoor project does not disrupt your life in the way that an indoor kitchen remodel would. Your family will function just fine for a month or more while an outdoor counter sits in the backyard in various stages of construction. There is a downside to the inessential nature of the project, of course: it allows you to succumb to procrastination.

Before you decide to jump in and build the whole thing on your own, interview yourself carefully.

■ **What is your skill set?** Many of the tasks shown later in the book can be learned, and we will teach you how. But it is best if you have a résumé that includes at least a

few modest home-improvement projects. If you have no experience with plumbing and wiring, review books like *Ultimate Guide: Plumbing* and *Ultimate Guide: Wiring* from Creative Homeowner. You may decide to consult a professional and perhaps hire one for these jobs.

■ **Do you have the time?** A modest counter might be buildable in a couple of weekends. But a number of projects, like running utility lines, making your own countertop, or constructing the housing for a pizza oven, will combine to take much more time than that. If working on them might seriously compromise your quality of life, it may be best to hire them out.

BELOW All of the techniques for building the counter shown here are covered in this book. Taken step by step, none are beyond the reach of a handy homeowner.

OPPOSITE A project with plumbing, electrical lines, and granite tops may be beyond your skill set; check the relevant sections of this book to be sure.

Dealing with Inspectors and the Building Department

It may be fine for you to build a counter and perhaps an overhead structure without benefit of a permit, as long as it is not attached to the house and does not have utility lines. If you will run electrical cable, plumbing pipes, or gas pipe, however, most building departments will want to know about it and watch over the process in a systematic way.

You might be able to get away with building an outdoor kitchen without first contacting the local building department if it will not be visible from the street. Doing so, however, involves some significant risks. If you are caught building something that should be inspected, you can get into legal trouble. When you sell your house, it may become apparent that you built the structure without a permit, and you may get into trouble at that point.

But most importantly, the building department and its inspectors are there to make sure that procedures are performed correctly and that no dangerous installations occur. Though they may seem picky and

perhaps even obnoxious, inspectors are there for your safety and the safety of your neighbors, and it is a good idea to follow their requirements.

If you plan to work with a contractor, have him or her deal with the building department. Otherwise, go to your building department for an initial meeting, bringing along a drawing of your project and a list of the materials to be used. They may have a printed brochure that answers most of your questions; if so, read it thoroughly and try not to bother the inspector with unnecessary questions. Learn about the sort of final drawings they need.

Depending on the department and local ordinances, you may be required to hire a licensed professional to run the wiring or the plumbing or both.

There will likely be separate inspections for wiring, plumbing, gas, and even the structure. Be careful about scheduling the inspections. Make sure that you do not cover up anything that the inspector needs to see until he or she signs off on the work.

3

Kitchens That Succeed

This chapter puts stunning outdoor kitchen projects on display. Some are simple and quite inexpensive, while others may stretch your budget or skill set. In any case, there are a plethora of ideas that you can borrow and incorporate into your own design. The projects come from all sorts of climates, and many have survived years of use in severe heat, cold, rain, and snow. The materials and techniques for building them are covered in later chapters.

Side by Side

Here is a great layout for people who like to entertain and create impressive food displays. In a relatively small space, there are two generous countertops—plenty of room for laying out a buffet or potluck settings. Of course, this much granite can be costly, but see pages 60–63 and 168–79 for less-expensive options.

The cooking-and-preparation counter takes a 45-degree turn to make space for a gas grill with modest countertop space on each side. Putting the grill at an angle like this makes it more convenient for reaching the other, long counter space. And the grill is a comfortable 6 feet away from the nearest stool, so diners will not get smoke in their eyes, while the cook need take only a step or two to reach them. The space between the two counters is 4 feet, which is optimal for maneuvering and serving.

The eating counter is one wide cantilevered slab, with ample room behind the dinner plates for arranging serving platters and bowls.

TOP A counter space like this can hold over a dozen serving platters or large bowls. The pergola post helps break up the space visually and hides electrical cable for the receptacles and refrigerator.

ABOVE The pergola is made of nicely joined cedar 4x6s stained a dark color. Because they are widely spaced, they offer little shade—mostly decoration and a fun place to hang things.

TOP The dining countertop overhangs the counter by about 16 in.—plenty of knee room. Four stools fit comfortably at the counter, with space for more serving bowls at the end.

ABOVE The counters were made using treated lumber, though they look like solid stone until you open a door. After framing the structures, the builder trimmed the door and drawer openings with white PVC pieces and then butted the faux stone to the trim.

Outdoor kitchen shown designed and built by Justus Lambros, Signature Decks

Handy and Neat

This design offers simplicity, economy, and ease of installation. Its crisp, tidy lines go well with composite decking or vinyl siding. For convenience, openings and recesses take the place of doors and drawers, putting everything in clear sight and within reach.

The contractor made the counter by building a simple wooden frame, then covering it with ½-inch white PVC bead-board sheets, which have a cottage look but are easy to wipe clean. He used PVC trim pieces as well. (See pages 146–49 for how to work with PVC sheeting;

you may choose instead to simply build the cabinets out of ¾-inch PVC sheets, as in this project.)

The counter is long, with a 90-degree bump-out at the end. The bump-out is about 6 feet from the dining table, making it an ideal buffet serving area. The 1-inch-thick granite is reasonably priced, and you could easily cut your own pieces if you located some remnants or used slabs. The backsplash is simply a piece of 3-inch-wide granite. Granite professionals attached it using a hidden metal splice, but you could instead attach it using extra-strong epoxy or polyurethane adhesive.

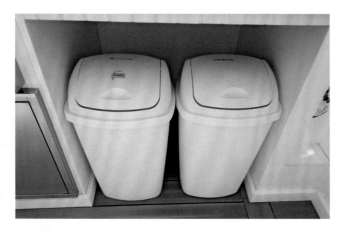

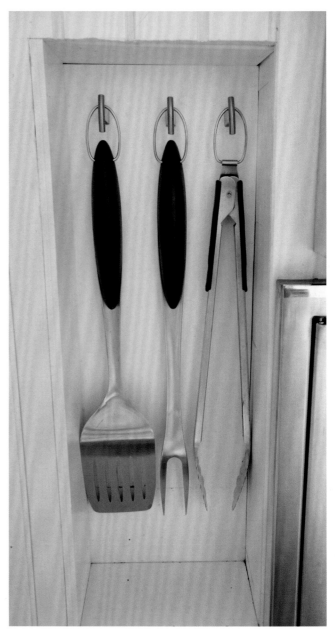

TOP There is only one set of access doors, just below the grill. A simple opening provides a place for garbage and recycling bins—white plastic containers that coordinate with the PVC and really do not need to be hidden.

ABOVE White bead board on the back of the unit coordinates seamlessly with the deck's white railing and trim.

RIGHT What could be simpler? On each side of the grill, a 12-in.-wide recess with three hooks puts tools or towels on display.

Outdoor kitchen shown designed and built by Gus DelaCruz, Barrett Outdoors

Blending In

An outdoor counter can add a dash of unexpected style to a backyard. Or as shown here, it can be carefully crafted to coordinate unobtrusively with the house. The latter approach will give even a small counter the appearance of solidity and permanence. This counter features faux stone siding that matches the pillars against which it nestles. It was built at the same time as the deck, so the decking was installed with picture-frame pieces traveling around the counter. This further enhances the feeling that the counter really belongs rather than being an add-on.

TOP RIGHT The light, speckled granite slab contains colors that coordinate with the stone facing below.

RIGHT For even more coherence, the builder mortised the counter into the pillar at the time of construction.

Outdoor kitchen shown designed and built by Gus DelaCruz, Barrett Outdoors

Minimalism

If you have modest cooking aspirations and storage
needs and are happy with your cart grill, a simple built-in
counter can create a pleasant and practical place around
which to gather with a few friends as you prepare food.
If you have a deck with a railing, simply widening the
railing may do the trick. Here, an inexpensive charcoal
grill/smoker can be rolled up to the widened railing

This railing is made of redwood, which you need to
lightly stain and seal unless you want it to turn gray.
Apply a high-quality water-based product or mineral
oil to keep spills from staining the wood.

**The railing was widened using 2x4s installed on
edge, with ¼-in. spacers between them.**

Outdoor kitchen shown designed and built by Bob Kiefer, Decks by Kiefer

Eating and Serving Counter

Instead of incorporating a grill into a counter, you may choose to build a pair of counters for serving and dining. This project has two long granite counters, each about 16 inches wide. The eating counter is about 42 inches high, and the serving/preparation counter is a standard 36-inch-high working surface.

You will find instructions for building this feature on pages 186–87. Pages 128–33 cover installing the faux stones between the pillars. The structure is simple to frame, but you must anchor it securely to the deck framing.

TOP With this arrangement, the cook can chat up the diners while preparing and serving the comestibles. The dining table in the background is about 10 ft. distant—just a few steps away, but in a clearly defined area.

ABOVE Support pillars, needed to lend rigidity to this narrow structure, are positioned to accommodate three nicely spaced stools.

Outdoor kitchen shown designed and built by Clemens Jellema, Fine Decks, Inc.

Two Big Curves

OK, the huge granite slabs make this one a stretch for a book on affordable options, but it definitely has features you can incorporate into a more modest design.

The counter is made using stackable block, which, as pages 156–59 show, is inexpensive and can easily be formed into a curve shape.

Two semicircular counters make for an intimate setting but also allow plenty of room for the cooks. At its widest, the distance between the two counters is about 7 feet, and on each side there is a 4-foot-wide space between the two.

The curves make granite more expensive. (The front counter was cut out of a slab over 5 feet wide.) But you could build a poured-concrete top instead, using a piece of composite decking to form the curved side. Or you could try to find some fairly inexpensive granite and cut it yourself. (See pages 58–59 and 162–65.)

Stackable blocks form curves with ease. The blocks that span over the door opening were simply joined together with adhesive; a hidden 2×4 lintel supports the grill.

Outdoor kitchen shown designed and built by Gus DelaCruz, Barrett Outdoors

Kamado-and-Gas-Grill Combo

In a small space, this counter incorporates a gas grill, for quick-and-easy cooking, and a kamado grill, which imparts charcoal flavor and gives the option of smoking or high-temperature pizza and bread cooking. (See page 37 for more information on kamados.)

The cabinets are made of PVC sheeting, as shown on pages 146–49. This material is stong and non-burnable, and it will remain easy to wipe clean for years. The doors and drawer faces are made of single ¾-inch PVC sheets, for a clean, modern appearance.

The L-shape allows the cook to easily operate one or both grills at once. Smaller counters like this that have appliances can use smaller pieces of granite, so you may be able to find large-enough remnants at a stone yard or from online listings (either new from retailer and manufacturer Web sites or secondhand from other online sources).

Outdoor kitchen shown designed and built by Justus Lambros, Signature Decks

TOP LEFT Doors are attached using self-closing Euro-style hinges. A special fold-down door allows access to the kamado grill's ash cleanout tray.

ABOVE If you are confident of your skills, you can make the circular cutout yourself using a grinder with a diamond blade. The inside edge of the cut will not show, so a belt sander can smooth it sufficiently.

LEFT CENTER An ice cooler is easy to accomplish when building with PVC: just make sure the joints are tight; use waterproof glue; and pour the ice right in.

LEFT BOTTOM As the sun goes down, the kamado grill glows and light from a nearby window glints seductively off the stainless-steel grill.

BELOW A door at the back of the counter provides storage for towels, used by those soaking in the nearby spa.

Stony Curves

Made of a limestone countertop and stackable concrete blocks, this counter has a consistent silvery gray hue that is subtly enhanced by a few light-rose-colored blocks. The result is a neutral canvas for showing off your fine dinnerware and colorful fruits and vegetables.

The contractor made the counter using stackable block, but you could make it using studs, backer board, and faux stone instead.

The counter is an acute L-shape, ending in a rounded dining area. This makes the space where the cook stands feel like a partial enclosure. The area near the grill has a backsplash with an 8-inch-wide ledge on top, just the right size for potted plants or cooking utensils. The eating peninsula has room for four or five diners, depending on how cozy they want to get. Unless there is an unfortunately directed wind, all of the diners will be just out of the range of the cooking smoke.

Design specifications usually call for an eating counter to be positioned 42 inches high, but this one stays at the same 36-inch height as the rest of the counter, so the diners and cook are all on the same plane. The arrangement requires tall chairs rather than conventional bar stools.

The countertop is made of Indiana limestone with a "rock" faced edge and sandblasted top. In most areas of the country, this option is considerably less expensive than polished granite. It commonly comes factory-sealed, but you may want to apply more sealer at least every year to keep it stain resistant.

Cutting Limestone

TIP

You can cut this kind of limestone using the granite-cutting techniques shown on pages 162–66. Cutting a curve like this and roughing it up can easily be done using a grinder. In fact—believe it or not—limestone can be cut using a reciprocating saw with a masonry blade. There is no need to keep the blade wet as you cut, though you may need to buy several blades. Just take your time, and continually check that you are cutting straight up and down.

Outdoor kitchen shown designed and built by Eric Weishaar, Breckenridge Landscape

A More Expansive Approach

Here the same materials are used but on a more monumental scale. The taller eating-table height carries through to become a ledge atop a backsplash behind the cooking area. On the other side (right) a limestone bench angles slightly away from the counter.

RIGHT Rough-edged limestone makes a handsome and solid-feeling outdoor counter.

BELOW The stackable-block construction features a row of blocks that are of slightly different color and protrude an inch or so for a roughly sculpted effect.

A Happy, Speckled Place

This L-shape counter features eating space for five and ample food-preparation room around the grill. A unique pergola decorates the area with dappled sunlight.

This kitchen is on the large side, but the design is kept simple and the appliances and doors are fairly minimal. The counter is made of wood studs, backer board, and faux stone. One wood and two pairs of stainless-steel doors offer access to the inside. The gas grill is modestly sized, which makes it suitable for casual dining rather than elaborate cookery.

The overhead structure, or pergola, is a head-turner. It starts with cylindrical columns, which can be purchased pre-made from online sources. Atop the columns sit massive 4×12 cedar beams, which give the appearance of having fancy joinery but actually just butt together. On top of the beams are 2×12 rafters. Topping the whole thing off are sheets of rusty metal artfully cut by a craftsman in a sort of wild, leafy, oblong-polka-dot pattern. (Cutting holes like this can actually be done without too much trouble using a rented plasma cutter.)

Outdoor kitchen shown designed and built by Justus Lambros, Signature Decks

TOP LEFT During the summer, diners are often clad in swimming gear, fresh from a dip in the nearby pool.

TOP RIGHT The overhead structure manages to be massive and playful at the same time, combining giant lumber pieces with an artfully perforated metal awning.

LEFT CENTER Rustic metal brackets provide a bit of support for the counter's knee-space overhang but are mostly there for casual charm.

LEFT BOTTOM In an unusual arrangement, the countertop was raised to 38 in. to satisfy a tall husband, and the grill was lowered to 34 in. to make it easier for a short wife.

BOTTOM CENTER Black hardware and the diamond pattern in the center dress up this simple wooden door. The patio floor is plain concrete, but the counter is so stunning as to make it seem charming.

BOTTOM RIGHT This stone frog seems at home on the semi-rough cultured-stone countertop. A surface like this may be called "honed" or "Venetian." Though not shiny, it is easy to wipe clean.

Classic Entertaining Centers

If you like to throw parties for a half-dozen or more couples from time to time, consider installing two widely spaced counters. A layout like this will make you more popular than ever.

At the end of the patio, just off the kitchen door, the L-shape cooking counter boasts a large grill, five access doors for storing a full set of kitchenware and implements, and counter space large enough that several people can work side by side. Two planters, a curved bench, and a straight bench create the rounded-L-shape conviviality area, which accommodates about 12 people.

The eating bar sits about 20 feet from the cooking counter. It faces the house wall, which holds a flat-screen TV and sound system. On game days, this can be a raucous sports bar; at other times, it can be an intimate place to watch movies or soaps with a few close friends and some delicious drinks.

All of the counters are made with wood cabinetry, built much the same as the project shown on pages 150–55. For a more cost-conscious approach, you might consider building with cedar rather than the Brazilian hardwood shown. But either way, you will have a stunning party venue.

Outdoor kitchen shown designed and built by Bob Kiefer, Decks by Kiefer

TOP LEFT Natural woodwork with a dark stain contrasts handsomely with the natural stone patio pavers. Some of the pavers have ruddy tones that nearly match lighter colors in the wood.

TOP RIGHT This granite is a popular pattern that is reasonably priced. Its multicolored speckles create a soothing backdrop for almost any other color. The large wood doors offer plenty of storage.

RIGHT This is a happy place both for imbibers and the bartender. The bar hides a refrigerator and a cooler, as well as enough shelving to satisfy the most ambitious of mixologists.

BELOW Thick uprights made of laminated 2×4s support the benches, and 2×4s and 2×2s with ¼-in. spacers between the pieces make up the seats.

Cozy but Open

This U-shape double counter—one level for eating and one for cooking—is surrounded by an airy wooden structure made of latticework walls and a soaring overhead pergola. The space forms a clearly defined room yet remains open to the world.

The wooden surround—both a lattice wall and an overhead shade structure—is made of cedar posts, beams, rafters, and top pieces. The builder cut the lattice from vinyl sheets, which are available in an attractive cedar tone. The lattice could have been wood, but staining (and re-staining every year or so) would have been a painstaking task; the vinyl looks great after a quick hosing.

The builder framed the counter using wood studs and covered it with composite decking, a material that looks much like natural wood but is nonflammable and easy to wipe clean. He used granite with a slightly rough surface and a rock-faced edge for the countertop. This material is only slightly more difficult to wipe clean than polished granite, and it hides dirt better. The light color ensures that it will not overheat in the summer sun.

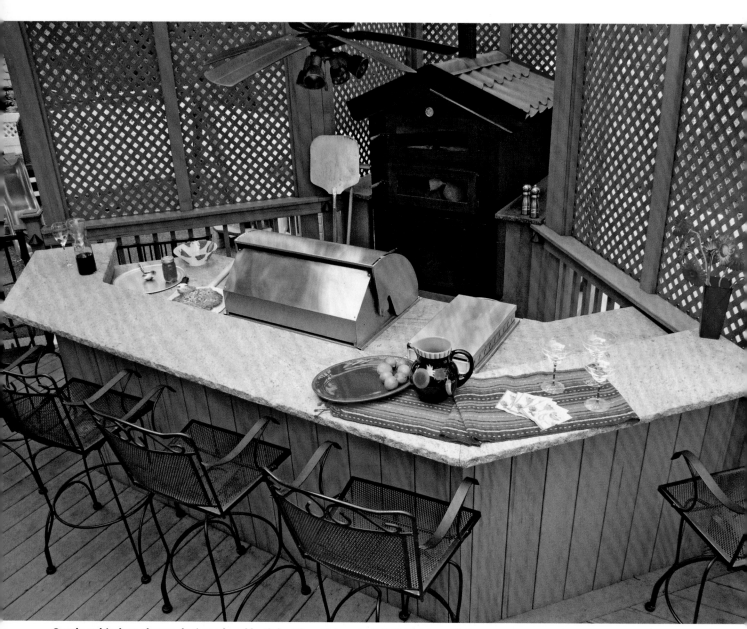

Outdoor kitchen shown designed and built by Dino Mazzone, D & M Outdoor Living

TOP LEFT The countertop's textured and honed surface produces a stony look and emphasizes the grains and striations of the natural granite.

TOP RIGHT The countertop's upper level overhangs enough so that diners can cozy up and lean on it without bumping their knees. The angled shape makes for a more convivial setting than a straight counter would.

LEFT CENTER The wood-fired pizza oven is an old-fashioned metal model that you can simply buy and put in place; there is no need to build a surround for it. It easily achieves temperatures of over 600 deg. F for crunchy breads and pizza crusts.

ABOVE The counter's easy-to-clean composite decking face blends well with the natural cedar decking below.

LEFT BOTTOM Overhead rafters with decorative end cuts, topped by 2×2 lattice, deliver partial shade from the afternoon sun.

Open Craftsmanship

If you like the look of turned posts and don't mind having open spaces for most of your storage space, here is another minimalist approach that may suit your tastes perfectly.

The kitchen fits nicely into a 9-foot-long bump-out in the deck. The railing is 36 inches tall, so the counter is flush with the railing's top cap. The big expense here is a massive 48-inch-wide gas grill, positioned so that there is about 2 feet of counter space on one side and 3 feet on the other. Below the grill is a short wooden counter made in much the same way as the one shown on pages 151–57. Of course, a simpler cabinet type would work as well.

The granite shows both speckles and veins, in tan and beige hues. The woodwork is all redwood, carefully stained and finished to closely match the ipé decking.

Outdoor kitchen shown designed and built by Bob Kiefer, Decks by Kiefer

ABOVE The granite top is at the same level as the railing's top cap, which helps integrate the counter with the deck.

RIGHT The builder made these turned legs on his own lathe out of 6×6 redwood, but you can order legs from a home center or from online sources.

Even Simpler

This approach not only saves money and effort but enables an outdoor kitchen to blend effortlessly with a deck and railing that has simple, modern lines. Here we see a substantial grill with integrated drawers that was made to be built into a counter. But you could also use a cart grill: remove its wheels, and build a simple frame around it.

The 4×4 posts and 2×4 horizontal countertop supports are the same materials as those used for the deck's railing. The countertop is about 2 inches lower than the railing's top cap, which creates what amounts to a low backsplash.

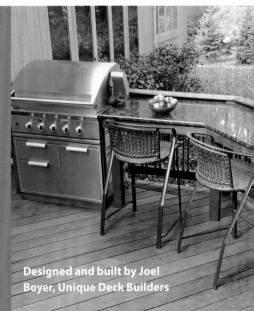

Designed and built by Joel Boyer, Unique Deck Builders

4
Building Counters

The best way to cut costs for an outdoor kitchen is to build it—or part of it—yourself. This chapter shows building the counter; the next deals with countertops and appliances. Most of the procedures are discrete tasks that you can tackle one at a time. The step-by-step instructions will enable you to build beautiful, sturdy surfaces even if you have never worked with stucco, tile, or poured concrete.

At every stage of the process you have myriad options for customizing the project to your needs. You may choose a stucco counter with a concrete top, a wooden counter with a tiled top, a tiled counter with a granite top, and so on. You may or may not install plumbing or electrical service; you can decide on the type of grill and burners; you can install stainless-steel or wood doors, a drawer unit, a refrigerator, or an option like a cooler or kegerator.

Small to medium counters with countertops take two or three hard-working weekends to finish. Construction will not disrupt your life much, so you will have ample time to make modifications as you go.

Detailed Planning

Once you have decided on the basic dimensions and appliances you want, start drawing. If you have a computer-aided design (CAD) drawing program or other design software, use that. But an outdoor counter is small and simple enough that you can achieve good results with graph paper, a pencil, and a straightedge.

Make at least two drawings: an overhead view of the countertop and a straight-on view of the counter's front. If the sides or back of the counter will have cutouts, draw them as well. When you come closer to actual building, you will draw a framing plan (page 118).

Drawing will help you spot and solve problems ahead of time. Some things to look out for:

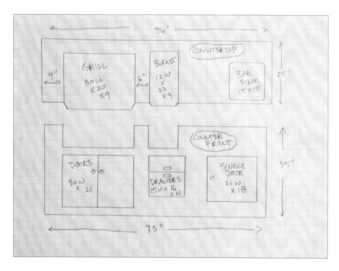

- **Be sure that you know where the smoke will go.** If you are installing under a porch roof, you probably need a strong range hood that will suck all of the smoke out and away.

- If you are planning seating, **position diners and tipplers well away from the grill**—at least 16 inches. It may seem like a nice idea to have an eating counter just opposite the grill, but all of that cooking heat—and smoke—can make the place very uncomfortable.

- **Provide an absolute minimum of 9 inches**—12 to 24 inches is better—**of counter space on each side of a grill or burner for food preparation.**

- **The bottom of door openings are typically 3 inches above the floor**—the thickness of two 2×4s. (Do not go any lower, or the door's flange will come very close to touching the deck or patio.) The clearance allows for easy access to the inside and creates a barrier that keeps out rain and snow. You can raise a drawer unit higher than 3 inches.

- If the counter turns a corner or is near the house, **be sure that all of the doors can swing open fully** and that any drawers can be pulled out all the way.

- **See that a sink has ample access below for the plumbing.** There should be a wide door (or pair of doors) below the sink so that you can install (and later, service) the supply and drain lines.

- If you will use propane tanks for a grill and side burner, **have a wide, accessible space below so that you can change out tanks easily.** You will also want room for an extra tank so you can keep grilling when one tank runs out. It is common to have a set of double doors about 30 inches wide below a propane grill.

- **Place any electrical receptacles where they will be easily accessible** but out of harm's way. You may need to install a receptacle inside the cabinet, for instance, for a refrigerator or a tankless water heater.

LEFT TOP Simple overhead and side-view drawings help you visualize the counter layout so that you can place things conveniently and save on materials.

LEFT BOTTOM This straightforward counter has ample counter space on each side of the grill; a tall, easily cleaned backsplash; and a well placed fridge.

The Floor

The counters we show in this chapter weigh a good deal less than a counter made of concrete block, so you don't need a thick reinforced-concrete footing. A solidly constructed deck or patio will do fine.

Have a large adult jump up and down on the deck where the counter will go, and check for noticeable bounciness. If you see movement of any kind, it is a good idea to beef up the framing, perhaps by attaching a "sister" joist alongside an existing joist. Similarly, if jumping on a patio causes pavers to rock, reset them as needed to make the area stable.

In most outdoor kitchens, the deck or patio functions as the floor within the counter. Even with the best-built counters, the floor will get wet after a hard rain. A deck should have ample drainage between decking boards. A patio should be sloped so that water runs away from the house, or it should have sand-filled gaps between the pavers so that water can drain.

LEFT TOP Well-sealed hardwood decking is easily cleaned and makes a practical kitchen floor.

ABOVE A dry-laid patio made of brick or other masonry will be strong enough to support most counters as long as the masonry is laid on a well-tamped sand-and-gravel base.

LEFT BOTTOM This patio floor is mortared onto a concrete slab, making it strong enough to support even an extra-heavy counter.

Some Basic Dimensions

- **Counter Height.** It is common for outdoor-kitchen countertops to be 36 inches above the floor, just as in an indoor kitchen (with the counter at 34 inches tall and a 2-inch-thick countertop). A dining or cocktail counter—which is sometimes installed alongside the food-preparation counter—is often 42 inches tall. You may want to experiment, however, by sitting on the stools of your choice to determine which height will be most comfortable. If you have extra-tall or -short people in your household, you may want to adjust the heights up or down by a couple of inches.

- **Countertop Width.** A standard countertop width (the distance from front to back, also called its depth) is 25 inches, but this is certainly not a hard-and-fast rule.

Granite tops often jump in price if they get wider than 25 inches. A tiled or concrete top can be as wide as you like with little effect on your budget.

- **Countertop Overhang.** The countertop should overhang the counter by at least 1½ inches, as in indoor kitchens, so you do not have to lean inward as you prepare food. A dining or cocktail countertop should overhang by at least 14 inches for knee space. An interior kitchen counter almost always has a toe-kick space at the bottom, but that may not be necessary for an outdoor kitchen.

BELOW This tiled countertop is only 24 in. wide, so it can be covered with two rows of 12-in tiles. Backsplashes with raised ledges increase the usable space.

What to Do Yourself?

Though it is small, building a counter calls for a surprising variety of skills. Read through the instructions that apply to your counter and decide which tasks you want to do yourself and which you may want to hire out. Operations that are definitely do-it-yourself (DIY) friendly include:

- **Building the counter's frame** with wooden or metal studs and cladding it with backer board
- **Applying stucco to the counter**
- **Applying ceramic or stone tiles to the counter**
- **Applying stone or faux stone to the counter**
- **Making a countertop out of ceramic or stone tiles**
- **Making a rough pour-in-place concrete countertop**
- **Constructing simple cabinets** out of wood or PVC
- **Attaching sinks and a faucet** and making basic connections for the under-sink trap and supply lines

Other operations might require you to learn new skills, and you may decide that hiring a professional would be more cost-effective. More-challenging tasks include:

- **Making electrical hookups for receptacles, lights, and appliances**
- **Running plumbing supply and drain lines**
- **Building a wooden cabinet** that features some fine woodworking
- **Cutting and installing a granite countertop** (though in some cases, as we will show, this can be a DIY project)

BELOW Granite countertops, gas hookups, and electrical wiring may be above your skill set, or you may choose to learn the needed techniques.

ABOVE AND BELOW Applying stucco (above) and framing with metal studs (below) are two examples of building methods that are surprisingly doable. Instructions later in the book will show you how.

Utility Lines

If you have basic plumbing or wiring skills, you may choose to run the lines yourself, perhaps consulting books like Creative Homeowner's *Ultimate Guide: Wiring* and *Ultimate Guide: Plumbing.* Or hire a professional to run the utility lines and make the hookups at the house, while you make the hookups at the counter. Be sure to obtain permits and schedule inspections as required.

If you need to run the pipes and cables underground, codes may require that they be buried at least 12 inches deep. For short runs you may be allowed to run the lines aboveground.

Electrical Lines

If you will install lights and receptacles that will use only a small amount of electricity, you may be able to tie into an existing electrical circuit by tapping into a nearby outdoor receptacle or junction box. If you plan to use heavy-duty appliances, however, it is best to run cable back to the electrical service panel and install a new circuit breaker. (See pages 124–25 for how to run conduit and cable for a GFCI, or ground-fault circuit-interrupter, receptacle.)

PVC (polyvinyl chloride) or metal conduit is often used for protecting electrical lines. You can run conduit all the way, or you might be allowed to run unprotected UF (underground feeder) cable at least part of the way.

Water-Supply Pipes

If you will have a sink with a faucet, you may choose to run only a cold-water line and hook that up to the faucet. This will allow you to rinse vegetables, though it will limit your cleaning possibilities. Another option is to install a small in-use (tankless) water heater inside the counter. Branch the cold-water line inside the counter, and attach one side to the heater. If the distance from the house is less than 20 feet, however, most builders believe that it is best to run both cold- and hot-water lines from the house. Wrap the pipes with insulation to prevent heat loss. (See pages 190–91 for instructions on installing a sink and faucet with plumbing inside the counter.)

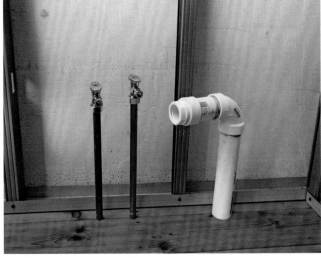

LEFT This trench carries a PVC drain line; copper supply tubing (just one tube, for cold water only); gray PVC conduit for the electrical line; and black pipe for the gas line.

ABOVE To prepare for a sink, run supply lines into the inside of the counter near where the sink will be. Add stop valves. (You may choose to run only a cold-water line.) Also run a drain line. Inside the counter, add an elbow, a short length of pipe, and a trap adapter, which accepts the drain trap. (See page 191.)

Working with Water-Supply Pipe

Today the three most common types of supply pipe for outdoor use are solid copper, CPVC, and PEX. Use the type approved by local codes. Here are some very basic instructions for assembling them.

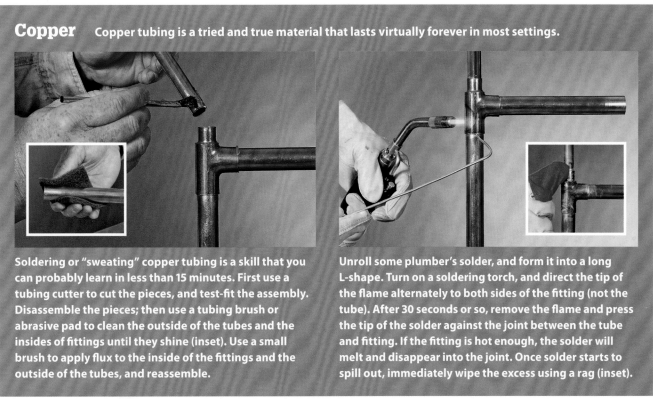

Copper   Copper tubing is a tried and true material that lasts virtually forever in most settings.

Soldering or "sweating" copper tubing is a skill that you can probably learn in less than 15 minutes. First use a tubing cutter to cut the pieces, and test-fit the assembly. Disassemble the pieces; then use a tubing brush or abrasive pad to clean the outside of the tubes and the insides of fittings until they shine (inset). Use a small brush to apply flux to the inside of the fittings and the outside of the tubes, and reassemble.

Unroll some plumber's solder, and form it into a long L-shape. Turn on a soldering torch, and direct the tip of the flame alternately to both sides of the fitting (not the tube). After 30 seconds or so, remove the flame and press the tip of the solder against the joint between the tube and fitting. If the fitting is hot enough, the solder will melt and disappear into the joint. Once solder starts to spill out, immediately wipe the excess using a rag (inset).

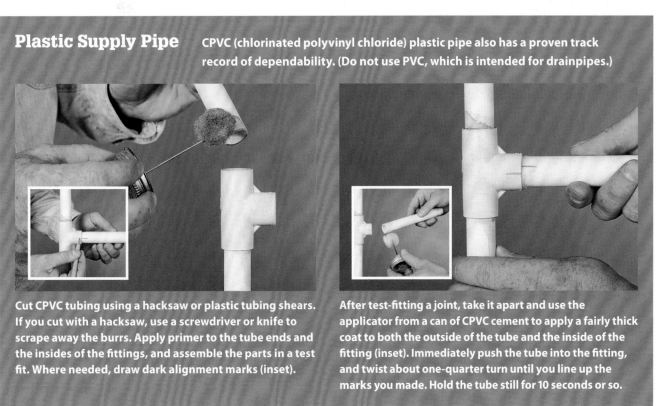

Plastic Supply Pipe   CPVC (chlorinated polyvinyl chloride) plastic pipe also has a proven track record of dependability. (Do not use PVC, which is intended for drainpipes.)

Cut CPVC tubing using a hacksaw or plastic tubing shears. If you cut with a hacksaw, use a screwdriver or knife to scrape away the burrs. Apply primer to the tube ends and the insides of the fittings, and assemble the parts in a test fit. Where needed, draw dark alignment marks (inset).

After test-fitting a joint, take it apart and use the applicator from a can of CPVC cement to apply a fairly thick coat to both the outside of the tube and the inside of the fitting (inset). Immediately push the tube into the fitting, and twist about one-quarter turn until you line up the marks you made. Hold the tube still for 10 seconds or so.

Pex Tubing

Cross-linked polyethylene tubing, referred to as PEX, is commonly used in many areas but banned in others. Do not use it if the tubing will be exposed to direct sunlight because ultraviolet (UV) rays can degrade it.

Cut PEX using a plastic tubing cutter (inset). (Your color of tubing may differ.) A great array of fittings allows you to join to other pipes and branch out. To attach fittings, slide on a crimp ring; slip the tubing over the barbed connector; then secure the crimp ring using a crimping tool.

Fasten the tubing at least every 2 ft. using plastic tubing brackets. Be sure to keep the tubes out of harm's way. At the end of the run inside the counter, attach the tube to a securely anchored copper stubout (inset).

Running the Drainline

PVC is the nearly universal choice for drainpipes. (See opposite for working with PVC.) When running PVC, follow local codes, which can be very specific. Make sure that horizontal runs of pipe slope downward at a rate of ¼ inch per running foot. If the drainpipe runs to the house's main drain, you may need to supply a vent pipe or use an air admittance valve (AAV) if that is allowed.

Trenching

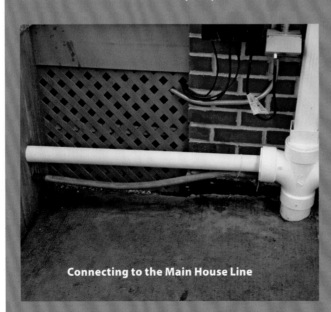

Connecting to the Main House Line

Running to a Dry Well

PVC Drainpipe

Connecting PVC drainpipe assemblies is a similar process to that for connecting CPVC, except that you must use primer and solvent cement formulated specifically for PVC.

Cut PVC pipe using a hacksaw, as shown, a handsaw, or a miter box. Make the cut square so that it is perpendicular to the pipe. Use a knife, file, or de-burring tool to remove the burrs (inset).

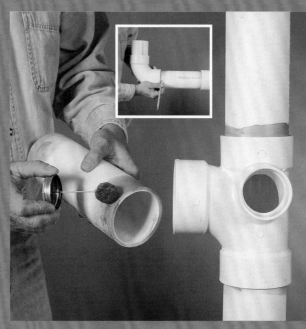

Apply primer to the end of the pipe and to the inside of the fitting using the applicator attached to the can's lid. Assemble several pieces in a dry run, and make layout marks where needed to maintain correct alignment (inset).

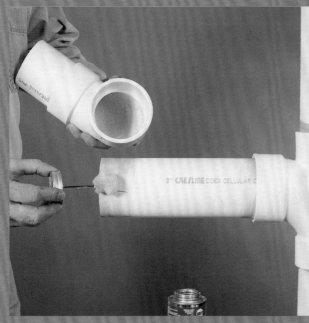

Disassemble the pieces, and prepare to work quickly. For each joint, apply PVC cement to the pipe ends and to the inside of the fittings.

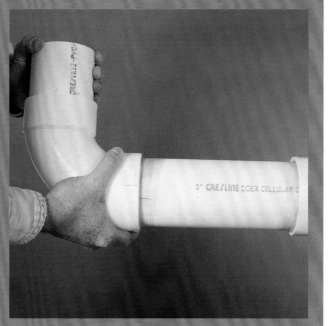

Push the parts together so that they are slightly out of alignment, and then twist and push until the marks line up. Hold the pieces in place for 10 seconds; then move on to the next joint.

Installing an Exhaust Hood

If your grill will be located inside a porch with a roof, the first question to ask is, Where will the smoke go? A grill generates much more smoke than an indoor range, and it will build up in a hurry, chase people away, and leave the porch area dirty over time. In this situation you will need an exhaust hood.

Unfortunately, a powerful-enough exhaust hood will set you back quite a bit of money; rearrange your outdoor kitchen, if possible, so that the grill does not need one.

If you have a roof but a large open vertical space behind the grill, you may not need an exhaust hood. Experiment by cooking with a cart grill in the place where the new grill will go. Cook up the smokiest, smelliest thing you can—perhaps blasting a chicken at 500 degrees F or so. If the atmosphere becomes uncomfortably smoky, then you need a range hood.

You will need a heavy-duty model; a standard $100 range hood will not do the job. Choose an exhaust hood that is at least 6 inches wider than the grill it will vent. It should pull air at a rate of at least 900 cubic feet per minute (cfm). It will require a lot of power, so you may need to install a new electrical circuit for it.

The ductwork needs to be done correctly so that air can move freely. Use smooth, solid metal ductwork rather than flexible, ribbed ducts, which slow down airflow, and configure it with as few turns as possible.

Framing a Counter with Wood

Even professional outdoor kitchen builders often build their counters using wood framing. Unless you have reason to believe that your grill or burner will get excessively hot, building with wood will not cause a fire hazard. Wood is easy to work with, especially if you already have carpentry skills.

Most of the wood framing will rarely, if ever, get wet, but it is a good idea to build with pressure-treated lumber to be safe. (Treated lumber costs only a bit more than untreated.) As shown in these steps, 2×4s are the most common choice. If you need extra room inside the cabinet, however, you could build using 2×3s or even 2×2s. The backer board that you will attach to the framing will supply a great deal of strength. Plan stud placement so that you can attach a full-length piece of backer board (which is usually 60 inches long). Locate joints in the middle of studs. If you will encase the inside of the grill opening with backer board (as shown on page 69), take into account the thickness of the board (usually ½ inch).

Select lumber that is straight. Minor imperfections like knots and checks will usually be covered, but if a board is bowed or twisted, it can make building difficult, and the result may be noticeably curved.

Here we show attaching fasteners using a pneumatic nail gun, a tool that has come down in price enough to make it fairly common among homeowners. You could also drive screws using a drill; this will be slower but will make disassembly easier if you make a mistake. Hand-nailing is also possible but can be awkward at times because it causes the structure to shake as you pound.

In most cases you can skip building a separate floor for the counter; just let the existing deck or patio surface serve as the floor. That way, when a bit of rainwater seeps in (as it almost certainly will), it can easily drain away. If you do make a floor, use pressure-treated plywood, and bore some drainage holes. You may also need to cut grooves in the bottom framing plate so that water can escape.

If your grill requires a metal sleeve, be sure to take that into account when planning the framing. (See page 192.)

For Wet Situations

Pressure-treated lumber rated for use *above grade* will be long lasting and rot free even if it sometimes gets wet. If the counter will rest on a surface that is often wet, so the counter's bottom will be soaking for days at a time, however, use lumber rated as *ground contact* for the bottom plate. Or use composite decking, which is absolutely rot resistant. You will need to rip-cut the decking to 3½ inches wide.

The Importance of Accuracy

At every joint, take care to hold the front of the stud perfectly flush with the front of the plate and perfectly aligned with your layout marks before driving a fastener. A mistake of even ⅛ inch may mean that a door or grill will not fit.

Figuring Length and Width

When determining the width and length of the counter, keep in mind that your countertop will likely overhang on all sides by 1½ inches or so. Also take into account the ½-inch thickness of the backer board that will cover the framing, as well as the thickness of your finish material (perhaps ½-inch-thick stucco or tiles with mortar). In a common configuration, the framing is 5 inches narrower and shorter than the countertop (1 inch on each side for backer board plus finish material and 1½ inches on each side for the countertop overhang). Also, you will make the side frames 8 inches narrower than the desired rough width of the counter because they fit between the 3½-inch-wide framing of the front and back (plus 1 inch for the backer board. (See page 119, Step 8.) Visualizing with a drawing makes the calculations easier.

Framing a Counter with Wood

• Measuring tape and pencil • Power miter saw or circular saw • Carpenter's square and angle square • Level • Power nailer, drill-driver,

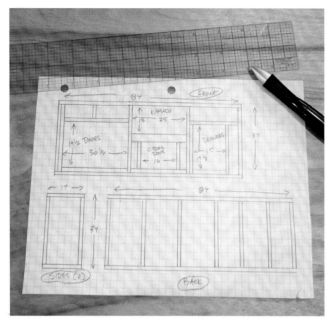

1 Make a framing drawing that shows the location of each framing piece. Make the openings the exact sizes given by the manufacturer for your grill, burners, drawers, and the like. First draw the vertical studs that will run from the bottom to the top plates (front and back). Then add horizontal pieces for the openings; lastly, fill in with shorter verticals.

2 The studs are 3 in. shorter than the desired height of the counter framing. In this case they are 31 in. long because there will be two 1½-in.-thick plates (top and bottom) plus a 2-in.-thick countertop, for a total countertop height of 36 in. Make a simple jig, as shown, so that you can cut all of the pieces to the same length.

5 Continuing to check for square as you work, cut and attach the interior horizontal and vertical pieces. Add a second row of horizontals at the bottom so that the doors will be raised up 3 in. Keep all board faces flush, and check openings for the right size. (See "The Importance of Accuracy," page 117.)

6 As a final check and for peace of mind, uncrate the components around which you have framed (drawers, doors, and the like), and place them into the openings to make sure that they fit.

3 Cut the top and bottom plates to length. (See "Figuring Length and Width," page 117.) Place them side by side, and using your drawing as a guide, lay out the locations for the full-length studs. Double check, especially for the front framing, to be sure that the studs are the correct distance apart for your openings.

4 Build the front frame first. Position the plates with the layout marks facing each other. Position studs at the marks, and double check to be sure the distances are correct. Place a framing square at one corner to keep things square as you work. Drive nails or screws to attach the studs.

7 Assemble the back and side framing. (Note that here the back wall is framed so that a 5-ft.-long piece of backer board will come flush to the end of the framing on one of its sides and fall in the middle of one of the studs on its other side.)

8 Set the framing sections upright, and check that they are square to each other. Drive nails or screws to attach the side studs to the front and back. Check to be sure that the tops of the framing sections are flush with each other before driving fasteners.

Framing with Metal Studs

Homeowners often shy away from metal studs, but they are inexpensive and surprisingly easy to work with. Standard metal studs, made of 20-gauge steel, are strong enough for most projects. If you will have an unusually heavy countertop, you may want to spend more for thicker 18-gauge steel. In this project we use 2×3 studs, which are 2½ in. wide; 2×4 studs would add more strength.

If you have a large project, you may choose to cut studs using a power miter box equipped with a metal blade, and perhaps attach them using a special crimping tool. But for a small project, cutting with aviation shears works just fine.

By itself, the metal framing is wobbly and unstable; once the backer board is attached, the counter gains greater stiffness. Here we show installing the backer board as you build the frame. For more instructions on cutting and attaching backer board, see pages 126–27.

Wear heavy-duty gloves when working with metal studs; the edges are quite sharp.

Framing Details

If you have a backsplash, an attached eating counter, angled corners, or other features, the framing can get complicated. The photos below demonstrate some of the methods used. The good news is that you can easily unscrew and disassemble connections if you make a mistake. You may want to hire a professional if you feel you are getting in over your head. Some principles to keep in mind:

- Double-check your openings to be sure doors and appliances will fit. Always keep in mind the thickness of the countertop material as well as the backer board and the stonework or stucco finish material.
- It may not always be feasible to attach backer board as you go. When framing without backer board, add temporary angled supports to keep the structure rigid (below left).

- When framing for a 45-degree-angle corner (below center top), here for an eating counter, run one of the pieces a foot or so longer than needed. Snip the long piece's two sides at the two points necessary to form the correct angle, and bend the piece to shape. Slip the longer angled arm over the piece coming from the other direction, and attach it using screws.
- When framing a cantilever, you may need to snip cutouts to accommodate the outwardly extending studs (below center bottom). (The framing shown here and in the photo above is fairly stiff but not strong enough to support the eating counter; it will be supported later by decorative angle brackets.)
- Adding backer board will actually supply much of the counter's strength (below right). Many builders prefer fiber-reinforced backer board to cement-based board for intricate framing with narrow openings.

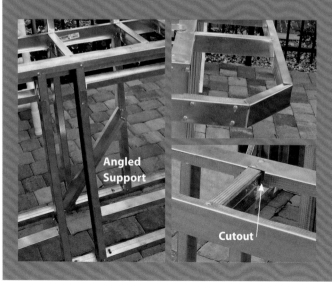

Angled Support

Cutout

Framing with Metal Studs

• Measuring tape and pencil • Aviation shears • Drill-driver • Framing square and angle square • Level • Metal studs •
Metal channels • Self-tapping screws • Cement-based backer board • Backer-board screws

1 Basic metal framing parts: a stud (right) is usually positioned vertically, and slips into a channel (left), usually positioned horizontally at the bottom and top. Fasten them together using self-tapping screws (bottom). Draw your framing plan (page 118, Step 1), and buy the pieces you need.

2 To make a basic cut, measure and mark the stud or channel using an angle square. Cut the sides (top). At this point you can either bend the piece back and forth a few times to finish the cut or cut the center portion using aviation shears (bottom).

3 To screw pieces together, use your hand to clasp the parts firmly, so the stud is tight up against the channel. Drive the screw through both the channel and the stud. If you have trouble, you may drill pilot holes first. With a bit of practice you can do without the pilot holes.

4 Working on a flat surface, build the back wall first. Position the studs 16 to 24 in. apart. Because you will attach 60-in.-long backer board, however, position one of the studs so that a full piece will fall in the center of the stud. Use a framing square to check that the assembly is square.

Continued on next page

Framing with Metal Studs, cont'd.

5 Cut the first piece of backer board to the height of the framing. (See pages 126–27.) Position it on the face of the rear wall, and attach it by driving backer-board screws every 6 in. into the studs and channels. Use the factory edges of the backer board as a guide to keep the wall perfectly square.

6 Following your drawing, cut the front-wall channels and full studs, and assemble them. Check and double-check your openings to be sure that doors and other components will fit.

8 Add the horizontal pieces with flaps, checking and double-checking the openings as you work. Drive screws through the flaps and into studs to attach them.

9 Stand the front framing section upright; hold a sheet of backer board against it; and mark from the inside for the cuts. Cut the openings using a grinder with a masonry blade (inset), and attach the backer board to the framing.

7 Around doors and under the grill you will need to install some horizontal framing pieces in the middle of studs. Cut a channel 3 in. longer than the opening, for a 1½-in. flap on each side. Mark the channel with lines indicating the actual opening. Snip two V-shape cuts (top); then cut off the edges (bottom).

10 Build side frames. (They will be narrower than the desired rough width of the counter by twice the thickness of a stud plus backer board thickness.) Position the front, back, and sides against each other; check that the assembly is square; and drive screws to join the side framing to the front and back. Add the side backer-board pieces.

Filling in at an Opening's Bottom

At the bottom of a door opening, regular framing will leave you with an open channel where debris can collect. To solve this problem, fill in with upside-down channels. Cut a channel in the opposite way shown in Step 7, cutting off the large flap so that you end up with two smaller edge flaps (below). Attach the upside-down channel by driving screws through flaps (bottom).

Wiring a Receptacle

There are a number of ways to run wiring into a counter, depending on your situation and local codes. Here we show one of the most common, installing metal conduit and running non-metallic (NM) cable through it. You may instead install PVC (polyvinyl chloride) conduit, which you assemble much the same as PVC drainpipe. (See page 115.) You may choose to run individual wires through the conduit instead of cable. Some codes allow you to run underground feeder (UF) cable and avoid installing any sort of conduit.

Plan the total run, back to the electrical service panel or to a nearby receptacle or junction box. Be sure that the new appliances you plug into the receptacle will not overload the circuit.

If your countertop will have a backsplash, you may choose to locate the receptacle there. Installing one onto the side of the counter, as shown in these steps, is another common choice.

Wiring a Receptacle

• Conduit and fittings • NM cable or individual wire • Outdoor

1 Assemble the parts you need to run to the junction box or service panel. For this situation, we use an outdoor-rated box with weatherproof compression fittings that connect to an elbow, which will connect to conduit.

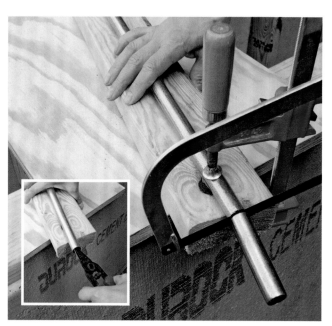

4 Clamp conduit tightly to a scrap piece of wood, and cut it using a hacksaw. Then use a special reaming tool or wire-stripper pliers (inset) to scrape away all of the burrs, which could nick the wire insulation.

5 Assemble the conduit and fittings, tightening each joint to keep it waterproof, and run it through the holes you made.

electrical box with all-weather cover • GFCI receptacle

2 Install framing to securely hold the electrical box and allow for the conduit. Here, a simple 2x4 is attached to wood framing. For an outdoor receptacle, you don't need to have the box end up flush with the counter's finished surface; this box will protrude about ½ in. from stucco or tiles.

3 Attach the parts shown in Step 1, and drive screws to secure the box to the framing. In this situation, the conduit is run down through the deck. You may need to run it out the side or perhaps through a trench in the lawn. Drill holes as needed, and measure the lengths of conduit runs.

6 In this case, the conduit runs under the deck. Use conduit straps to hold it tightly against framing members.

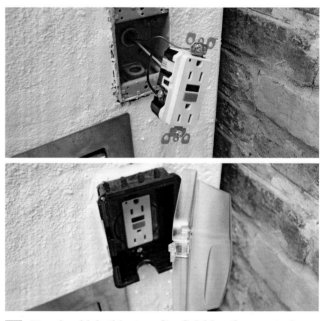

7 You should do this step after finishing the counter's sides. Run the cable or individual wires to the junction box or service panel. Shut off the power. Wire the receptacle (top); then make the connections at the other end. Add an in-use cover (bottom), which protects the receptacle from rain even when something is plugged in.

Adding Backer Board

Most counter siding materials—stucco, tile, stone, or faux stone—require a substrate that remains durable when wet. The nearly universal choice is cement-based backer board, or cement board (or cement backer). There are two basic types: cement with an embedded fiberglass mesh and fiber-cement, which has fibers running through it. Attach it using special backer-board screws. Use 1⅝-inch screws; shorter screws may not fasten securely.

Backer board is heavy. If you are worried about the counter's weighing too much, you could use pressure-treated plywood instead. It will work in most situations but is not quite as solid or durable as backer board. You can also use an exterior gypsum-based sheathing product. (See page 185.)

Cutting standard cement-based backer board is usually described as being much the same as cutting drywall: slice through the mesh on one side using a utility knife; snap the backer board back; and slice through the mesh on the back side. It is not nearly as easy to cut as drywall, though. When you need to make a cutout, we recommend using a power tool.

If you choose fiber-cement board, cutting with a utility knife will be slow work indeed. Use a special hand cutter or a grinder with a masonry blade.

Avoid Little Pieces

TIP

For greater strength as well as greater ease when applying the stucco, tile, or stone finish, make careful cutouts from a large piece of backer board rather than cutting small pieces and narrow slivers. Handle the cutout sheet carefully when installing it because you can easily break it until you attach it.

Adding Backer Board

- Cement-based backer board • Measuring tape, pencil,
- Backer-board screws • Grinder with masonry blade

1 Backer board is typically 3 ft. wide, and the countertop is usually a few to 9 inches narrower than that, so you will likely begin with a long rip cut. Use a pencil and straightedge or a chalk line to mark for the cut. Score a cut along the line deep enough to slice through the fiberglass mesh. A deep-enough cut may require two or more passes.

4 To mark for a cutout, hold the sheet in place and use a pencil to mark from the inside of the cabinet. Hold the pencil at an angle so that it draws a rectangle that is about ⅛ in. larger than the actual opening to ensure that none of the backer board protrudes into the cutout area.

chalk-line box • Utility knife (with plenty of blades) or backer-board cutter • Drill-driver with screw and ½-in. masonry bits
• Saber saw with masonry blade

2 Snap the backer board along the line you just cut. You may be able to make the break using your hands, but if the cut is near the edge of a board, as it is here, you will probably need to tap the waste piece using a hammer and a piece of scrap board.

3 Rock the waste side back and forth a few times to better expose the fiberglass mesh on the other side. Cut through the mesh (from either side of the board), and pull the piece apart. Use the utility knife to clean away any large bumps in the cut edge.

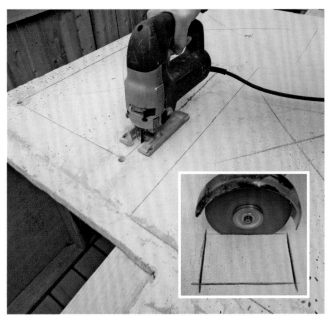

5 To make a cutout, position the sheet so that it is firmly supported while you work. Drill holes at the corners with a masonry bit and then cut using a saber saw with a masonry blade. Work slowly to avoid overheating the blade. Or you can make the cuts using a small grinder equipped with a masonry-cutting blade (inset). Finish the cuts from the other side.

6 Hold the sheet in place, and drive backer-board screws into framing members. Drive the screws so that they just barely indent. If you drive them too far, they will break the surface and not hold as well; too shallow, and they will become obstructions when you apply mortar or stucco. Drive screws every 6 in. into each framing member.

Applying Stone or Faux-Stone Veneer

Once you have attached the backer board, you can face the counter with a variety of finish projects. We start with stone veneer. This is certainly the most common type of siding for outdoor counters, so we devote several pages to it. Veneer stones may be natural stones cut thin for easy installation. Or as shown on these pages, they may be made of lightweight concrete with a stone appearance on one side. Manufacturers have become so adept at making faux stones that, once they are installed, most people cannot tell whether they are fake or not. If you go with natural stone, the installation method will be similar.

Some veneer stones come in one width only, so installing them is much like stacking bricks. Others, as shown here, come in various widths for a more natural look. This will be a more challenging installation. The stones will likely have two or three widths only, so you will probably not need to cut many stones lengthwise. Corner stones have an L-shape so that once installed, they produce the illusion of a thick stone surface.

Bring a drawing of your counter to the dealer when buying stones. A salesperson should be able to help you order the right number of stones for the field and corners. He or she may also help you choose a colorant for the mortar (grout) that you will apply in the joints between the stones. As shown in these steps, many people do not add colorant because the natural gray adds a classic contrast.

This project does not call for the skills of a mason, but it does require attention to detail, careful installation, and thinking ahead. Take your time, and stand back every so often to examine the work so that you do not end up with a wavy line of stones or too many stones of the same color clustered together.

The Right Mortar
Type-N mortar is probably strong enough for this project, but most professionals use Type-M, which is even stronger.

TIP

Applying the Stones

The time needed for applying stones varies widely, depending on the number of cuts you need to make (the more obstructions, the more cutting), the size of the stones, and whether or not the stones are manufactured to easily line up with each other.

A Helper Helps
On a project that needs numerous cuts, it can be tedious to continually get up and down to cut stones and install them. And on most projects, the stones should be cut a couple of yards away from the deck or patio to ensure against damaging it. If you can call out measurements or hand a marked stone to a helper with the grinder, things go more smoothly.

TIP

RIGHT Carefully installed stone or faux-stone veneer has the look of natural stone. The corners look as if they are made with large stones.

Applying Stone or Faux-Stone Veneer: Applying the Stones

• Faux or natural stone veneer (both field and corner stones) • Type-N dry-mix mortar • Colorant for the grout mortar (optional) • Masonry cement • Drop cloth • Wheelbarrow or mason's tub • Hoe or shovel • Pointed brick trowel • Round-nosed mason's trowel • Masonry jointer • Grinder with masonry-cutting blade • Measuring tape and pencil • Mason's hammer • Grout bag • Spray bottle • Mason's brush • Dust mask and protective eyewear

1 Arrange the stones on nearby drop cloths so that you can visually scan and easily choose among them. Arrange them according to size or color.

2 Pour an inch or so of water into a wheelbarrow or mason's tub. Pour in a bag of mortar mix; add more water; and mix using a shovel or hoe. Continue mixing and adding a little water at a time until the mortar is the consistency of mayonnaise. It should be quite wet and just firm enough so that it sticks to a shovel held sideways for a second or two before falling (inset).

3 If you are working on a deck or a patio with a smooth surface, protect it using pieces of cardboard or heavy construction paper. If the floor is bumpy, lay down ¼-in. plywood to create an even surface.

4 Draw lines as needed on the backer board to help you stay aligned. (Here, a centerline is drawn on a narrow section, and alternating courses will be placed with joint lines an inch or so on either side of the line. This helps ensure that the layout will not be too regular looking.)

Continued on next page

Applying Stone or Faux-Stone Veneer: Applying the Stones, cont'd.

5 It works best in most layouts to start at the corners. When measuring for cutting corner stones, you sometimes need to take into account the thickness of the mortar bed, which will hold the stone away from the backer board by about ³⁄₈ in.

6 You could cut stones using a wet masonry saw, but a grinder works well and allows you to shape the stone more naturally using small cuts. It creates a lot of dust, so wear a dust mask and make sure the wind blows away from you. On a drop cloth or lawn, stabilize the stone, and cut slowly. (Surprisingly, a diamond blade cuts masonry but does little damage to a boot.)

9 To ensure that a horizontal line of stones does not slope across the face of the counter, measure and mark guidelines (or story lines) at the corners (as shown) and along the face of the counter. You do not need to apply stones right up to these marks, but try to arrange the stones so that they generally follow the guidelines.

10 Once you have installed the corners, fill in the field with longer, flat stones. Apply mortar to the backs of the stones in the same way as with the corners, scraping to make sure the mortar sticks at all points and creating a ½-in.-thick ridge in the middle.

7 Do not apply mortar to the backer board for corners; it will only create a mess. Use a trowel to slather a thick coat of mortar onto the back of a corner piece (top). The mortar should be about ½ in. thick in the middle. Use the trowel to taper the sides as shown. Press the first pieces in place until mortar starts to squeeze out (bottom). You want mortar to stick to both the backer board and the stone at all points.

8 Work the mortar into the joints using a gloved finger (top); this will prevent voids and air bubbles. Then add a layer of mortar to the top of the stone, creating a base on which the next stone will rest (bottom). Work carefully so that no mortar drips down or smears onto the stone faces.

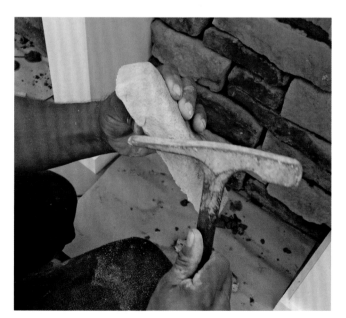

11 Pay attention to the layout lines as you work, and stand back from time to time to make sure that the stones form straight lines. If a stone has a small protrusion on its back, you can usually scrape or tap it away using a mason's hammer instead of grinding it down (box at right).

Scraping a Too-Thick Stone

If a stone has a bump on its back that needs to be removed or if it is so thick that it protrudes noticeably, you can cut back the raised area to reduce the thickness. Hold the stone in place to identify the thick area, and mark it using a pencil (below left). Then gently cut it back using a grinder, moving the grinder back and forth slowly to remove material as needed (below right).

Continued on next page

Applying Stone or Faux-Stone Veneer: Filling the Joints, cont'd.

Some stones (like dry-stacking stones) require no mortar, but most need to have joints filled. The product that fills the joints is

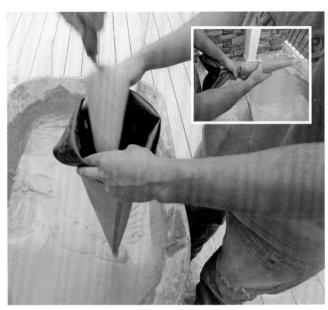

12 When you are ready to grout, pour a bag of mortar mix into a wheelbarrow or mason's tub; then mix in two shovelfuls of masonry cement (to ensure that it will stick to the sides of the stones). Add water, and mix to a thin, just pourable consistency. The resulting grout should slide off a shovel readily but not be so soupy that it will dribble down the face of the wall.

13 Use a trowel to scoop grout into a grout bag, filling it one-third to one-half full. Grab the back end, and twist to create a tight seal (inset); squeeze and twist until mortar just starts oozing out. Apply the grout to an inconspicuous place as a test; if it dribbles down the face of the wall, pour it back into the wheelbarrow and add some dry mix to stiffen the grout.

15 Where a joint is thin and the grout bag cannot squeeze in material, load a trowel with grout; slip it into the bottom of the joint; and use a thin jointing tool to push the grout in (top). Then use the grout bag. When the grout is stiff enough so that pressing a thumb leaves an impression that holds its shape (bottom), go to the next step.

16 Gently brush the surface using a mason's brush, taking care not to smear the stone faces. On a hot, dry day with the sun beating on the surface, this job may take only 15 min.; under other conditions it can take hours. If the grout is too wet, wait another 15 min. or so and try again. Fill in any voids with grout, and brush again.

basically thinned mortar, or grout.

14 Push the tip of the bag into a joint; then twist and squeeze until grout oozes out. Move the tip across the joints as you squirt (top). Fill the insides of the joints as you go; avoid getting grout on the stone faces. If the grout stiffens, add water. If it remains stiff, throw it out and make a new batch. When the bag gets clogged so that grout comes out in spurts, empty it and run water through it (bottom).

17 If the grout dries quickly, spray it with a fine mist of water to slow down the curing process. (The slower the cure, the stronger the grout will be.) Once the grout is dry, wipe the stone surface with water (inset). After a day, clean smears off the stone by brushing with a solution of one part muriatic acid to three parts water; wear nitrile gloves and protective clothing.

Globs and Smears
TIP

If you get a glob of mortar on the face of the stone, do not try to wash it off; doing so will create a smear. You can gently remove some of the grout, but do not press on it in any way. Allow it to mostly dry; then gently pry it off.

Larger Stones

Large faux stones are not as heavy as you may expect. Cut and install them in much the same way as the smaller ones. The joints will be less consistent in width than for smaller stones, but that only adds to the charm.

Applying Stucco

Common in some areas and rare in others, stucco is a tried and true siding material that, if applied correctly, will remain lovely and crack free for many decades, even in cold climates. And it is surprisingly easy, though time consuming, for a do-it-yourselfer to apply.

When covering a plywood-sheathed house, stucco is usually applied in three coats. On backer board, you need only two coats: a base coat and a finish coat. Wait a week or so between coats to achieve full strength. If you are in a hurry, you can buy a more expensive stucco mix that can be applied all in one coat and that cures more rapidly.

It may take an hour or so to get the knack of finishing a surface with stucco. You can practice while working on the base coat. By the time you apply the finish coat, you will know how to achieve the finish of your choice.

BELOW A great-looking stucco surface has a fairly consistently textured surface but does not need to be perfect. With a bit of patience and the right tools (especially a sponge float), you can achieve success.

Applying Stucco

• Stucco base-coat mix • Stucco finish-coat mix • Packing tape • Strips of foam insulation or scrap boards • Stucco corner bead
• Stucco stop bead • Sheets of stucco lath • Roofing nails • Aviation shears • Hammer • Wheelbarrow or mason's tub • Hoe or shovel
• 16-in.-sq. plywood • Flat trowel • Margin trowel • Sponge-type grout float • Grout sponge • Paint, paintbrush • Drill-driver, bits

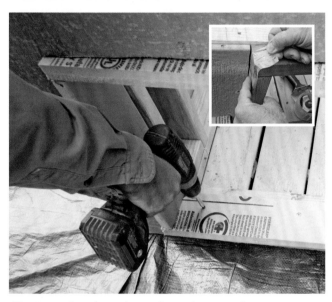

1 Around each untrimmed opening, attach temporary filler strips against which you can butt the stucco. Here we use thin pieces of rigid foam insulation. The foam has a slick surface to which the stucco will not stick. You can also use scrap lumber; spray the boards with oil first. If the stucco will butt against finished wood, protect it with packing tape (inset) or painter's tape.

2 Cut pieces of stop bead for the bottom of the counter and corner bead for the outside corners using a pair of aviation shears. Wear gloves; this material has sharp points.

3 Attach the stop bead, then the corner bead using roofing nails driven into framing members. Cut away the very bottom of the corner bead's lath portion so that you can align the bottom of the corner bead with the bottom of the stop bead to form a neat bottom corner.

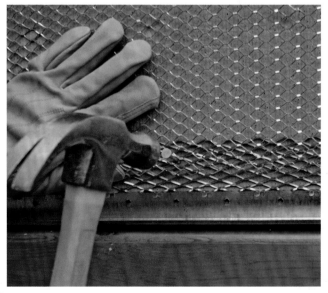

4 Cut sheets of metal lath so that they overlap onto the stop bead's and corner bead's mesh, and attach them using roofing nails. Hold the sheets flat against the wall as you work to prevent wrinkles and protrusions.

Continued on next page

Applying Stucco, cont'd.

5 Mix a batch of stucco base coat in a wheelbarrow or mason's tub. The stucco should be wet and just stiff enough so that it sticks to an inverted tool for a few seconds before sliding off.

6 Place a shovelful of stucco onto a piece of 16-in.-square plywood. Hold the plywood at the bottom of the counter; with a flat trowel, scoop up stucco; and then spread it onto the wall with an upward motion, pressing against the wall. Some stucco will fall; try to catch it with the plywood.

9 Where you must apply stucco to a narrow section, use a margin trowel or other narrow tool. Be sure that the stucco is the same thickness here as on the rest of the wall.

10 The slower stucco cures, the stronger it will be. A week of curing is ideal. Cover the stucco with plastic to keep it from drying too quickly. Also, spray the surface with a fine mist—just enough to dampen it—once or twice a day.

7 Once you have applied stucco to a large area, spread it using the trowel. Continue pressing as you work, and use long, sweeping strokes. Aim to cover most if not all of the waffle-like lines made by the stucco lath.

8 Use a sponge grout float to generally smooth the surface. Take this opportunity to practice your smoothing technique for the finish coat. (See the steps ahead.) Fill in any voids, and work to remove any protrusions.

11 After the base coat is cured, go over the whole surface, scraping away any globs and ridges that stick out (inset). Mix a batch of finish stucco, and apply it using a piece of plywood and a flat trowel, as in Steps 6 and 7. (The product shown is gray; yours may be white.)

12 To create a slightly rough surface, use a sponge grout float. Press gently, and use long, arcing strokes. With perseverance you can remove most waves and ridges and fill in any holes. In places too narrow for a grout float, use a grout sponge to achieve a similar texture (inset).

Continued on next page

Applying Stucco, cont'd.

13 Cure the top coat. (See step 10.) Remove all forms and tape; you may need to caulk some joints. Apply 100-percent acrylic or high-quality latex paint using a large brush and a poking motion to ensure that the paint fills all of the crannies. For the second coat, you can use a roller.

14 You could stucco right up to the underside of the countertop, caulk the joint, and paint carefully. But it is easier to leave a small gap and cover it with a trim board like this 2x2 cedar. Stain and finish the boards; drill pilot holes; then drive deck screws into a framing member.

Two More Textures

Professional stucco installers often apply distinctive textures that they have perfected over years of practice. You can produce a swirly texture with a mason's brush. Or try these:

■ Dip a mason's brush in stucco, and flick it at the wall to spatter it and produce a bumpy surface (below left). If you like these bumps, go over the entire surface a couple of times to achieve a reasonably uniform spatter pattern.

■ After spattering, you may prefer to scrape the surface very lightly using a trowel, which will flatten the bumps out and produce a classic "knockdown" texture (below right). Again, stand back; examine your work over the whole wall; and perhaps add more spatters to knock down as needed.

Facing a Counter with Tile

Once you have built the counter and installed backer board, finishing with tile is a pretty straightforward process. Rough-textured natural stone tiles are a popular choice, partly because they lend a nice outdoorsy feel and partly because you do not have to finish the edges. (If you want softer, more-rounded edges, use the methods shown on pages 164–65, Steps 9 and 10.)

You will use essentially the same techniques to apply stone and ceramic tile. Most ceramic tiles have edges that look unfinished if left exposed, however, so you may need to apply bullnose ceramic tiles at the corners.

Often, you can buy slate tiles like the ones shown on these pages at bargain prices. Less-expensive types are sometimes quite weak, even fragile; you may be able to break some with your hands. They will be strong enough for your purposes, however, once installed in a good bed of thinset mortar. As a bonus, the cheaper tiles are usually the most interesting to look at, with swirls and splotches of rust, tan, gray, and even purple hues.

You cannot cut stone tiles using a "snap" cutter made for ceramic tile. A masonry wet saw is the best tool. You can buy a modest but effective one for under $100. Or rent a better saw. You can make some cuts using a grinder or circular saw with a masonry blade, but the grinder will be slow going and mass cutting may produce enough dust to damage a circular saw.

Large, pockmarked travertine tiles face this counter's sides, making a classy yet neutral backdrop for the colorful countertop tiles.

Cutting a Notch

For an electrical box or other obstruction, you may need to cut a notch. Start by making a series of closely spaced cuts inside the overall cut lines (right). You can break the resulting slivers out using your fingers (below left). Finish the cut by gently rubbing the roughly cut edge against the spinning blade to scrape it smooth (below right).

Facing a Counter with Tile

• Slate tiles • Acrylic tile or masonry sealer • Tile spacers • Fortified thinset mortar • Sanded grout • Wet saw • Hammer • Measuring

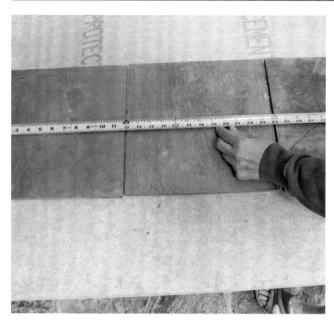

1 When measuring tiles for cutting, take into account the thickness of the grout joints. Use 3/16- or 1/4-in. joints when working with rough stone tiles.

2 Set up the saw to keep the blade wet at all times while you are cutting; otherwise, you risk dulling the blade quickly. Position the fence for the cut (inset), and slowly push the tile through the blade for a straight cut.

5 Place cardboard strips or thin plywood at the bottom, and press the tiles into the mortar, using the spacers to achieve consistent grout lines. Every few tiles, pull one away to see that mortar is sticking to at least 75 percent of the surface. If not, back-butter a thin coat of mortar.

6 Where you need to tile above an opening, screw a wooden guide strip to the underside of the upper part of the opening, and place the tiles on the strip. Stone tiles are sometimes irregular in shape, so you may need to use strips of cardboard as spacers in some places.

tape and pencil • Margin trowel and bucket • Square-notched trowel • Paintbrush • Sponge-type grout float • Grout sponge

3 Slate is porous, so grout that you have rubbed on it will be difficult to clean. Avoid this problem by applying acrylic masonry sealer to the top surface only—not the edges. If the sealer soaks in quickly, apply another coat. Allow the sealer to dry before installing the tiles.

4 Add dry-mix polymer-modified thinset mortar to water in a bucket. (If the mortar is not polymer modified, mix it with acrylic liquid as directed.) Mix the mortar to a mayonnaise-like consistency (inset). Apply mortar to the backer board using a square-notched trowel held nearly flat, and push the mortar onto the backer board. Tilt the trowel 45 deg., and comb the mortar for a consistent surface.

7 Place a small, straight board on the tiles, and tap it with a hammer to ensure that the tiles are firmly bedded. The tiles may be irregular. If a corner stands out too far, you may be able to tap it in. If part of a tile is too low, remove it and apply extra mortar as needed. Allow the mortar to harden overnight; then mix a batch of sanded fortified grout.

8 Press the grout into the joints using a grout float. Tilt the float, and moving diagonally, scrape away the excess. Dampen a grout sponge with water, and wipe away grout (inset). Do not dig into the joints. Constantly turn, then rinse the sponge. Change the water often. After wiping a few times, allow the grout to dry; then buff the tiles with a cloth.

Building Wooden Access Doors

A good-quality stainless-steel door (or set of double doors) will typically cost from $100 to $300. You can build a large, charming wood door using high-quality cedar and decorative outdoor hinges for less than $40. If you use ipé or other ironwood, the price will likely double.

A wood door is less weather-resistant than a steel door, but even the steel door does not reliably seal out rainwater. If you make the door out of dark heartwood and protect it well using sealer and stain, it will last for a long time.

Here we show building some basic doors using a modest set of tools. For a door that calls for finer woodworking, see pages 152–55, Steps 8–13 and 18. Wood doors for outdoor kitchens are typically flush, meaning that they are on the same plane as the surrounding jamb and there is a ⅛-inch gap between door and jamb all around. You can use simple decorative hinges, as shown here, or European-style hidden hinges, as shown on pages 149 and 154.

The door shown uses 2×4s for the perimeter and 1×6s for the interior. The result is a simple Craftsman-style look.

These doors were made with mitered trim all around and straight vertical pieces in the middle, following the steps on the next few pages.

Attaching Metal Doors

Typically, you install metal doors, drawer sets, and other units made for an outdoor counter by simply driving screws. Test the fit; you may need to scrape away some stucco or mortar. Apply a bead of caulk to the inside of the flange, and push the door unit against the counter (below left); if it doesn't seal at all points, pull it away and add more caulk as needed.

Unfortunately, most doors have inner mounting flanges that are not as wide as they should be, so the screw holes may be a bit short of the stud. In most cases, you can drive screws at an angle to catch the stud (below center). Or you may need to drill new screw holes. Use washers and stainless-steel screws for a firm grab. When driving screws into metal studs, take care not to overtighten, which could strip out the hole and cause the screw to spin. If that happens, drive a screw in another place.

A self-encased unit like a set of drawers needs a bit of support, which you can supply by attaching blocking to the deck or patio surface (below right).

Building Wooden Access Doors

• 1- and 2-by lumber as needed • Power miter saw • Table saw • Drill-driver with countersink bit • Wood glue
• Clamps • Stainless-steel or deck screws • Finish nail gun

1 Use a power miter saw to miter-cut the perimeter 2x4s to form rectangles the size of each door. Set up the table saw to cut ¾ in. deep, and position the fence 1½ in. from the outside of the blade. Make the first cutting pass, as shown. Cut all eight pieces this way (for the two doors).

2 Move the fence to be ¾ in. from the outside of the blade. If you are using ⁵/₄ decking instead of 1x6s for the back pieces (Step 6), make it 1 in. away. Holding the 2x4 on edge as shown, cut the second pass. For both passes, it is OK if the cuts are a bit too deep. Cut all eight pieces this way.

3 Equip your drill with a counterbore bit (inset). The bit's long shaft should be slightly smaller than the screw's shaft, and its counterbore should be slightly larger than the screw head. Apply wood glue to the inside corners.

4 Use a clamp to hold two of the pieces tightly together, with their surfaces perfectly flush. Drill a pilot hole in each direction. Be sure to offset the holes so that the screws will not run into each other.

Continued on next page

Building Wooden Access Doors, cont'd.

5 Drive a screw through each hole so that the head sinks into the wood ¼ in. or so. Use 3-in. star- or square-drive screws and a bit to match (inset). Drill holes and drive screws into all eight joints.

6 Cut the back pieces to fit—but not tightly: they should be about ¹/₁₆ in. shorter than the opening. Apply glue; set them in a bed of glue; and drive small finishing nails to hold them in place (inset). Or drill pilot holes and drive short screws.

7 Allow a day for the glue to dry; then fill the holes, and sand the edges. Here is what the door fronts look like. Install hinges, and attach them to the doorjambs as shown on the next page.

Simpler Wood Doors

For a more rustic look and not much work, consider this simple design. If you use cedar (as shown here), choose dark-colored heartwood, which will resist rot. (Light-colored sapwood can rot quickly.) First make and install a simple doorjamb, using 2x4s or 2x6s ripped in half (below left). Carefully check that the jamb frame is square, and use shims as needed.

Measure the opening, and cut boards for the door (below right). Here we use $^5/_4$ decking, which has round-ed edges that produce an attractive ribbed look. You may choose to use 1×6 pieces instead for a smoother face. Build a door that is $^1/_4$ inch shorter and narrower than the opening for a $^1/_8$-inch gap between door and jamb all around. Cut two cleats about $^1/_2$ inch shorter than the door. Position the cleats where you want to install the hinge so that you can drive screws into them. Apply wood glue, and drive two screws through the cleats into each board. Here, we use a temporary wooden guide to keep things straight and square.

Attach hinges to the door, positioned so that the hinge screws penetrate the cleats on the other side. Then use shims to hold the door in place, with a $^1/_8$-inch gap all around (bottom left), and drive screws to attach the hinges to the jamb (bottom left inset). Attach a handle or knob. For the latch, here we use a simple interior cabinet latch (bottom right). (You can use either a catch or the magnet type shown.) This latch might rust after a few years but will be easy to replace.

Building PVC Cabinets

Some lumberyards stock 4 × 8-foot PVC (polyvinyl chloride) sheets, and others can special order them. You can cut and fasten the sheets using standard carpentry tools. The cost is two to three times the price of plywood, but PVC produces no splinters when you cut and mill it, will not rot, and will need no finishing once assembled (though you may paint it if you want to). Polymer sheets have many of the same properties.

Use ¾-inch sheets to build the basic cabinets and the face frames. To make doors and drawer fronts like those shown here, use two layers of ⅜-inch stock.

Building cabinets like these calls for basic carpentry skills and careful planning. Start by making detailed drawings on graph paper or using a CAD (computer-aided design) or other software design program, and follow the drawings as you work to be sure that your grill and doors will fit.

RIGHT These frames, doors, and drawer fronts are all made with single sheets of ¾-in PVC stock for a clean and nearly seamless look.

Build the cabinets 4 inches shorter than you want them to be. Then install them onto 4-inch-tall toe kicks, which are simple rectangles 2 inches narrower than the cabinets. That will give you a 4-inch-tall toe space at the bottom of the cabinet.

PVC Drawers

To make a drawer, purchase drawer glides and follow their instructions for building a drawer box of the correct width. The drawer face will be ¼ in. smaller than the opening, just like the doors. Fasten the drawer boxes together using pocket screws or PV cement and nails or trim-head screws. Attach the glide parts to the cabinet and to the bottom of the drawer. You can use drawers creatively. A tall drawer, for instance, can hold one or two garbage bins (below left); a drawer that is tightly sealed with glue can be used as a cooler (below right).

Building PVC Cabinets

• PVC sheets, ¾- and ⅜-in. thick • PV cement made for joining sheets (not plumbing PVC cement) • Table saw or circular saw, rip guide
• Pocket screw jig • Drill-driver, bits • Pocket screws • Miter box or power miter saw • Router (with or without router table)
• Long clamps • Nail gun (or drill-driver and trim-head screws) • Euro hinges with screws • Forstner bit for Euro hinges

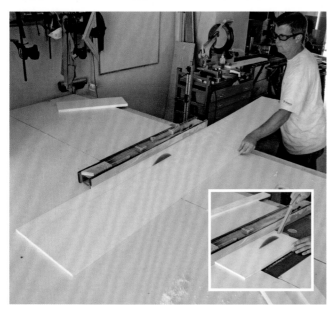

1 Cut the side, back, top, and bottom pieces using a table saw or a circular saw with a rip guide. Make the sides the width of the cabinet minus the thicknesses of the back and the face frame. Work carefully, and use a push stick (inset) to keep your fingers at least 3 in. from the blade.

2 Assemble the box using pocket screws (as shown on page 148, Steps 5 and 6), checking that it is square as you work. Fasten the sides to the top and bottom; then attach the back. Add any dividers. (Here, there is a double-thick vertical piece, which will support a kamado grill.)

3 Cut pieces for the face frame 2–3 in. wide using a table saw. The face frame should be ¼ in. wider and taller than the cabinet so that it runs past the cabinet ⅛ in. all around. Cut the pieces to length using a power or hand miter saw.

4 For the face frame, door parts, and other components, you may choose to ease the edges using a router. Here, we use a simple bevel bit. Routing edges is easy if you have a router table. It is not much more difficult using a handheld router as long as you use a self-guiding bit.

Continued on next page

147

Building PVC Cabinets, cont'd.

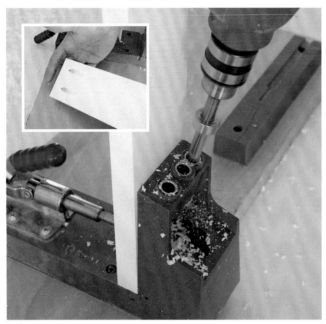

5 To fasten pieces using pocket screws, adjust the jig to drive screws at the correct angle for fastening ³/₄-in. stock, following the manufacturer's instructions. Clamp one piece, and drill a hole that goes nearly through its edge. The finished holes will have an oblong shape (inset).

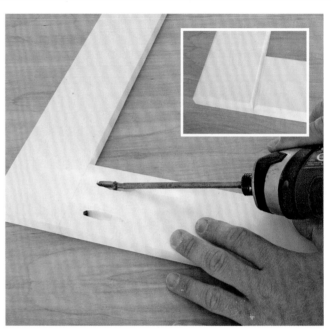

6 Position the pieces to be joined; use clamps when needed. Here we show attaching the back of the face frame. Using a long screwdriver bit, drive screws to fasten the pieces. The routed edges add a handsome detail to the front of the face frame (inset).

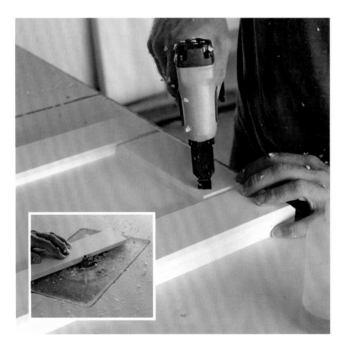

8 To make a door with a detailed look, use ³/₈-in.-thick stock. Cut a piece the full size of the door. Then cut narrow pieces for the perimeter, and bevel the front edges on all sides (inset). Attach the perimeter pieces to the full-size piece using glue and ⁹/₁₆-in. finishing nails.

9 Test the fit of the door; there should be a ¹/₈-in. gap all around. If necessary, cut the door to the correct size; then re-bevel the cut edges using a router.

7 Clamp the face frame onto the cabinet, and check that it is aligned all around. Drill pocket holes into the front edges of the cabinet frame so that they point toward the cabinet face frame. Drive pocket screws to fasten the face frame to the cabinet.

Painting Plastic

Many homeowners like the look of pure-white PVC sheets, but other colors may be available in your area. You can also paint PVC. Use paint specially formulated for use on plastic, or first apply adhesion primer and then apply high-quality acrylic paint.

10 To attach Euro-style hinges, drill a hole near the edge of the door using a Forstner bit. Slip the hinge into the hole; hold it parallel with the door edge; predrill; and fasten it (inset). Position the door in the opening; then fasten the other side of the hinges to the cabinet frame.

11 To make a counter, connect individual cabinets using screws. This counter is made of three cabinets. Build a 4-in.-tall toe kick using PVC; make it 2 in. narrower than the width of the cabinets, front to back. Set the cabinets on top of the toe kick, and attach it using screws.

149

Crafting Wood Cabinets

If you have a woodworking bent and some good tools, you can make an outdoor wooden counter in much the same way as an indoor one by crafting cabinets that support the grill and countertop.

The project here was designed and made by Bob Kiefer, a topflight New Jersey deck builder. Kiefer incorporates many fine details, including raised panels and posts that he lathes himself. You might choose to use some of his techniques but build simpler panels and doors.

Kiefer uses cumaru, a Brazilian hardwood that is a bit softer and more flexible than ipé, which has a tendency to crack when used for cabinetry. Cumaru is also somewhat less expensive than ipé. You could also build a cabinet out of cedar or redwood.

Make a scale drawing that shows the required openings for your grill, doors, and other features, and refer to it often as you work.

Using Poly Glue

TIP

Polyurethane glue works best when wood surfaces are damp. Before applying it, give both boards a quick spritz of water using a spray bottle.

BELOW This cabinetry uses more modern-looking square-cut rails that are butt- rather than miter-jointed, and the inside portions and drawer fronts are made of plywood.

Crafting Wood Cabinets

- Cumaru or other outdoor wood • Pressure-treated 2x4s • Power miter saw or miter box • Drill with countersink bit • Screws
- Hardwood plugs to fit the countersink bit • Polyurethane glue • Belt sander and random-orbit sander • Long clamps (10 or so)
- Router (and router table if possible) • Biscuit joiner with biscuits • Table saw • Turned posts • Chisel and hammer

1 A cabinet floor helps stabilize the structure and is a nice feature for the area behind a door. With this project, only the middle section has a door. (See page 155, Step 19.) Miter-cut three pieces of treated 2x4 and one piece of cumaru (inset) to the width of your grill minus 3 in. and the width of the counter (front to back) minus 3½ in. Drill pilot holes, and drive screws to attach the pieces.

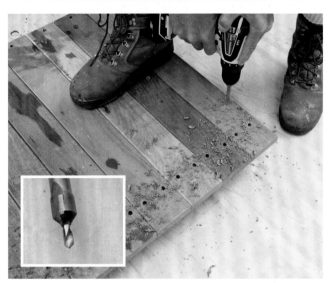

2 Cut pieces of cumaru to form the floor; they should be as long as the width of the cabinet, minus 1½ in. for the combined thickness of the face frame and the back panel. Position the pieces on the floor frame, flush to the edges of the frame, with small gaps between them. Drill attachment pilot holes using a countersink bit (inset).

3 Drive screws to attach the flooring to the frame. Drop a dab of polyurethane glue into each hole; then push in wood plugs. You can purchase wood plugs or make them yourself using a plug-cutting bit and a drill. The latter option might be better because you can make the plugs from matching cumaru. Wait for the glue to dry; then sand the surface smooth (inset).

4 Plan for a structure that will reach the desired height of the counter (in this case, 34½ in., for a total height of 36 in. once you have installed the countertop). Using pressure-treated boards, attach one upright at each corner of the floor. First drill holes up through the bottom of the floor; then drill angled pilot holes, and drive screws (inset).

Continued on next page

Crafting Wood Cabinets, cont'd.

5 Add crosspieces on top of the uprights (inset), and check again that the height is correct. Then attach a simple frame between them. Be sure the frame will support the grill at the desired height, taking into account the thickness of the countertop. (Some grills hang by their flanges onto the countertop; this type needs support underneath.)

6 Set the grill temporarily in place. Make sure that the countertop will slip in under the grill's flanges. Check underneath to be sure that electrical and gas connections do not bump against the framing (inset).

9 At the ends of the rails (the horizontal pieces) and the intermediate stiles (verticals), use the tongue-cutting bit to cut a tongue that fits into the groove (top). The bottom photo shows how the pieces fit together.

10 Determine the desired width of the panel sections, and cut a number of 1x6s longer than needed. Assemble them in order, numbering to keep track, and draw short lines across the pieces to use as reference points for cutting the biscuit grooves (left). Stack the boards in order. At each of the lines, cut a groove using a biscuit cutter (right).

7 With the grill still in place, build the face frame out of 3-in.-wide cumaru. (Here, there is a temporary spacer on the lower right, where the refrigerator will go.) You can attach these pieces using a biscuit joiner or by clamping them together, drilling long pilot holes, and driving screws. Add polyurethane glue, and clamp the pieces to dry.

8 The cabinet back, sides, and doors are made of frames and panels. The frames have grooves into which the panels will fit. You will need a router table and a three-piece *raised-panel door-making set* of router bits. Use the groove-cutting bit to cut grooves all along the inside edges.

11 Apply glue to the grooves and sides of all of the pieces in a panel section; insert biscuits and more glue (top); and push the pieces together. Use clamps to tighten the pieces (bottom). The photo shows clamping several panels at the same time. Put one clamp on top and one on the bottom for stability. Let the glue dry for a few hours.

12 Once the glue has set, use a table saw to cut the panels to the desired size. Keep in mind that once you have dressed the edges using a router (next step), the panels will slip into grooves in the panel frame (Step 14), so cut them ½ in. larger than the dimensions inside the frame.

Continued on next page

Crafting Wood Cabinets, cont'd.

13 Use the router table with the third bit in the *raised-panel door-making set* to cut the raised detail on all four sides. Once dressed, the edges will fit snugly into the grooves that you already made in the frame pieces. Use a random-orbit sander to remove the squeezed-out glue and smooth the panel face.

14 Assemble the rails and panels. Slip an end stile into the lower rail; then add a panel, then an intermediate stile, and so on. Tap using a block of wood rather than a hammer to prevent denting (top). Apply glue only to the rails at the corners; the panels should be able to move slightly with changes in temperature. Finish by adding the top rail (bottom).

17 Attach a cleat to the side of the cabinet, and drive screws to attach the horizontal supports from Step 16. Slip the supports into the post grooves; drill pilot holes; and angle-drive screws to fasten them. Miter-cut both ends of two angle-brace corner supports; drill pilot holes; and drive a long screw into each brace to attach it to the corner of the post (inset).

18 Build doors using the same method as you used for the back and side panels. Make the doors about 1 in. larger than the opening in both directions (to overlay by ½ in. all around). Using a Forstner bit and guide, drill holes for the Euro hinges. Set the hinges into the holes, and fasten them with screws. Hold the door in place, centered over the opening, and attach the hinges to the frame (inset).

15 Make the side panels in the same way as shown in Steps 5–9. Equip the router with a rabbet bit, and cut a rabbet groove along the inside edges of the side panels (inset). Attach the sides to the face frame and the cabinet back, and drive 4d finishing nails to fasten it.

16 Cut the horizontal boards that will tie into the posts you will use. (Store-bought cedar posts will do, next step.) Mark the post tops for grooves into which the horizontal boards will fit. Cut tight kerfs inside the marks using a circular saw; use a router with a straight bit to clean out the groove (inset); finish the corners using a chisel and hammer.

19 Fill any fastener holes; sand the entire surface; and apply finish. Set granite or another countertop slab in place, and set in the grill and refrigerator.

A Simpler Cabinet

This counter is made of a wood frame covered by T1-11 plywood siding, with straightforward wood trim at the top and bottom. It is not nearly as impressive as the cabinet we have just shown, but once finished with a granite-slab countertop, a classy grill, and stainless-steel doors, it is quite attractive. And you can build it quickly using basic carpentry tools.

Build a wooden frame as shown on pages 117–19; then mark the plywood for cutting as you would backer board (pages 126–27). Cut the plywood using a circular saw and saber saw, and screw it to the frame. Install a countertop and grill, and add the doors.

Stackable-Block Counters

Here is one of the easiest and fastest ways to build an outdoor counter. Stackable wall blocks simply stack on top of each other, gaining their strength from their interlocking indentations and protrusions. You need to apply adhesive only when attaching the countertop or top cap.

You can find companies that sell concrete block with the appearance of natural stone at home centers and masonry-supply centers and from online sources. In addition to selling patio pavers and retaining-wall blocks (which stack to lean into the soil they will retain), many companies also offer *wall block,* which stacks straight vertically. You can use these blocks to make a simple or complex outdoor kitchen counter. Once erected, you can top the structure off with any of the countertop options shown in the next chapter. You may also want to incorporate the company's cap blocks as part of the countertop.

Check the manufacturer's literature to select the correct type and number of blocks you will need. Typically you will need corner blocks, which have one finished end; regular field blocks; and split, or half, blocks.

Some blocks are installed in a *running bond pattern,* meaning a regular sequence of one block on top of two. In that case, there will be half blocks only at the ends of courses. Or you can install a *random pattern,* which uses a number of scattered half or fractional blocks along the length of each course for a more natural look.

Because the blocks are not mortared together, there is no need for a thick concrete footing that will resist frost heave or movement. Any relatively stable surface—a patio, a tamped gravel bed, or even a deck strong enough to support the weight—will do. The surface needs to be level and straight, however.

Cutting Block

TIP

You will need to cut some blocks. Cut first using a circular saw or grinder equipped with a diamond blade. To save the blade and reduce dust, have someone gently spray the blade with water as you cut. Once you have scored a cut line all around the block, whack it with a cold chisel and hammer to finish the cut.

BELOW This simple stacked structure has an opening where an inexpensive cart grill can be wheeled in.

Understanding Corners

When you have corners, you should always start building at one. With some products and patterns you can simply alternate full and half blocks to achieve a running bond. With others, you need to make some cuts.

1 Draw the counter's layout on the floor; stretch a mason's line; or simply follow your patio's or deck's lines. Lay a corner block with the finished end facing out. Cut a block to create one-quarter and three-quarter blocks. Put the cut end of the three-quarter block against the corner block.

2 Start the next course right away. For this second course, position the corner block at a right angle, or 90 deg., to the first-course corner block, with the good end facing out. Then lay the one-quarter block from Step 1 against it on top of the first block you laid.

Building a Curve
TIP

Some companies sell special blocks that have one face longer than the other. This makes it easy to build a curve. Mark a curved line on the floor, and install the special blocks with the long side facing out.

BELOW This style of stackable block is a bit smoother and has tighter joints for a more refined appearance.

Building a Stackable-Block Counter

1 Lay the first course, cutting blocks as needed to create corners. Create the full layout of the counter, and check that your grill and other appliances will fit in the openings.

2 Continue laying blocks. With most products, five courses of block plus a 1–2-in. countertop will add up to a standard countertop height of around 36 in.

3 Install the top course with all protruding features facing down so there will be a smooth surface to serve as the base for the countertop.

4 Order or make the countertop pieces. Once you are certain of the fit, apply a thick bead of adhesive, and set the countertop on it. (Polyurethane construction adhesive works well.) In some places you may choose to place cap blocks as shown.

This stacked-block counter unit allows room for a roll-in cart grill's built-in shelves.
See page 69 for more information on using a cart grill.

5

Installing Countertops & Appliances

As pages 60–63 show, there are plenty of reasonably priced countertop options, including ceramic or stone tile and poured concrete. Even granite can be surprisingly inexpensive, especially if you buy a slab and cut it yourself—a task that is surprisingly doable.

Working at the counter will be more comfortable if its top cantilevers beyond the counter by 2 inches or so. You can install the countertop after installing the counter's siding. In that case, you may need to add trim under the countertop to cover the gap between the stone or stucco and the top. Another approach is to install the countertop after installing the backer board. Then you can apply the counter's finish surface so that it butts against the countertop.

A granite slab top is strong enough to span the width of a 2-foot-wide counter by itself, but some installers install a backer-board substrate first to more fully support the slab. For other types of countertop, you will almost always need a backer-board substrate.

Granite and Other Slab Countertops

A granite slab has a substantial feel, great natural beauty, and permanence—and it is a snap to wipe clean. Quartz offers even better performance because you do not have to seal it. You can hire a granite company to install a countertop for you; many charge as little as $30 per square foot, though you will pay extra for sink holes and other cuts. On the next four pages we show how to cut and install a granite countertop yourself—saving a lot of money.

See page 60 for buying strategies. With a little buying savvy, you may be able to find all the granite or quartz you need for less than the price of a lesser countertop.

Transporting the slab might be the biggest challenge. If you get a ¾-inch-thick slab that is 6 to 8 feet long, two reasonably strong men can probably carry it without too much strain. If it is thicker or longer, arrange to move it with the aid of a few helpers or have it moved professionally. Another alternative: once you cut the slab to fit, it may be much lighter, so you might want to cut it before moving, if possible.

Cutting the material is surprisingly doable using a $35 diamond blade on a circular saw and dribbling water

on the blade as you work. You can sand cut edges smooth using a belt sander; if you need it to shine, you will need to buy or rent a wet grinder and a set of polishing wheels made for the purpose. You can also cut a hole for a self-rimming sink; if you want an under-mount sink with polished edges, hire a pro.

Cutting with a Grinder

TIP

You can cut granite using a grinder equipped with a diamond blade if the cut does not have to be perfectly straight. Here we show using a clamped board as a guide, but you can cut freehand if you are careful. Keep the blade wet as you cut. Make two or more passes of increasing depth.

BELOW A granite countertop with details like these angles and ogee-shape edging is a job for professionals. If it is what you want, check with local fabricators; the cost may not be prohibitive.

Installing a Granite Countertop

- Granite or quartz slab, from ¾ in. to 1½ in. thick • Framing square, measuring tape, and pencil • Circular saw with diamond blade
- Clamps and straightedge, such as a level • Grinder with diamond blade • Hose with spray attachment • Plywood for a hole guide
- Belt sander • Silicone caulk and caulking gun

1 Plan the layout carefully. It is common to have the countertop overhang the counter by 1–2 in. all around. (If you have not finished the counter sides, take into account the thickness of the finish material.) If possible, place any seams behind the cutout for a grill or other appliance, as shown here.

2 To make a straight cut, place the granite on at least four boards (two on each side) so that the waste will not fall when you complete the cut. Clamp a straightedge, such as a level, as a guide. Have a helper gently squirt water on the blade as you cut. It will take a few minutes to make a 2-ft.-long cut. Exert moderate pressure, and cut without stopping for a smooth edge.

3 When making a cutout or notch, keep the waste section well supported, and cut along the line in both directions. If the corner will be covered by a flange, you can run the cuts past the corner by ¼ in. or so. The waste piece should break out easily. If it does not, use a grinder to cut deeply at the corner in both directions.

4 To make a hole for a sink, cut using a grinder. You would probably be fine cutting freehand, but to be sure that the blade does not skip forward and damage the top as you work, cut and clamp a plywood guide, as shown. Hold the blade against the guide as you cut.

Continued on next page

Installing a Granite Countertop, cont'd.

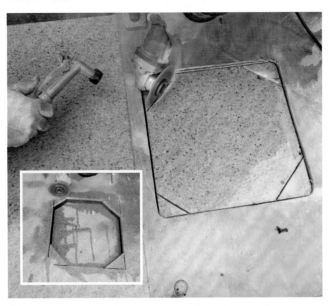

5 At each corner, cut short angled sections as shown. Keep cutting until the octagon-shape piece falls down (inset).

6 Continue cutting as much as possible at the corners. The pieces should break out by hand or with the light tap of a hammer; don't bang hard, or you may crack the top. If needed, make shallow cuts along the lines at the corners (inset); then tap the piece out.

8 If there is a seam, set both pieces in place, and make sure that you have correctly positioned them. Slide one of the pieces away by an inch or so, and apply a bead of clear or colored silicone caulk. (If you want a perfect color match, purchase custom-colored caulk from a granite supplier.) Push the pieces together, and wipe the seam with a solvent-dampened rag.

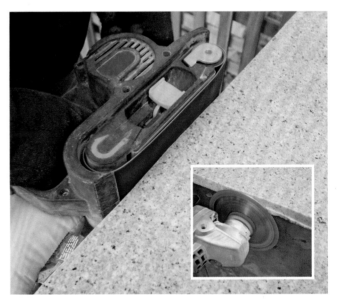

9 If a cut edge will be visible, sand it with a belt sander, using 60-grit paper. If there are substantial protrusions, carefully grind them most of the way down first (inset). Once you have sanded the edge smooth, switch to 80-grit paper and sand again. Repeat with 100-, 120-, and 150-grit sandpapers, and continue to increase grits until the surface is as smooth and shiny as you want.

7 Check that the top of the counter is smooth and free of protrusions. Carry the cut top to the counter; gently set it in place; and make sure that it does not wobble. If it does, remove it and lay down a thick bead of caulk to provide a continuous setting bed. Once you are sure of the countertop's position, run a bead of caulk along the underside against the counter.

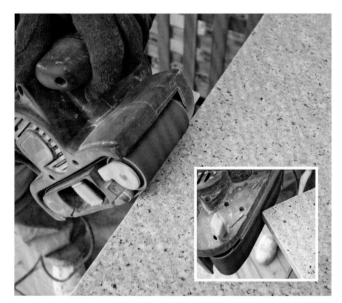

10 Use the belt sander to slightly bevel the top edge. Work slowly and carefully—do not press down— until the edge looks like a factory edge. At a corner you may choose to make the same bevel as on the other edges (inset), or you may continue sanding to make a more rounded edge.

Cutting Thicker Slabs

TIP

The steps on these pages show cutting a ¾-inch-thick slab. Cutting a thicker slab will of course be more time consuming, but the process will be much the same. The corners of a hole cutout will take more care. You may need to make a series of horizontal cuts up to the cut line to make it easier to break the pieces out.

Cutting a Curve

Cutting a curve in granite is not difficult. You can cut a gentle curve using a circular saw, but cutting with a grinder is easier. Make a simple trammel to mark for the curve. (See page 181.) Make a shallow cut along the line, pulling the grinder toward you rather than moving it away from you. When you deepen the cuts, use a straight-cut piece of 2x4 as a guide (below) to keep the cut square (straight vertical). Once you have finished the cut, use a belt sander to smooth the edge (bottom), starting with 60-grit sandpaper and moving on to progressively higher grits until you achieve a surface that is smooth enough.

Rough-Stone-Slab Countertops

If you have a rough stone slab like the ones shown below left and right and bottom left, you can cut it in the same way as a smooth one. You will need to roughen all exposed edges after cutting for a natural look. Different stones act differently, so test-cut a scrap piece, and get proficient before working on the real thing.

Make sure the slab is well supported on a flat surface to minimize the risk of cracking it. Use a grinder to slightly roughen the edge by lightly grazing in randomly spaced areas (bottom right). Pull the grinder toward you rather than pushing it away from you as you work. It may also work to gently tap with a hammer to produce a series of indentations. Take care: one false hammer blow could crack the slab.

Preparing a Countertop Substrate

To prepare for installing a flagstone, ceramic-tile, stone-tile, or poured-concrete countertop, as shown on the following 12 pages, you must first install a substrate. Plywood (preferably pressure-treated plywood) is sometimes used for this, but in most cases the best option is cement-based backer board.

- Cement-based backer board
- 2x4s for cross braces
- Screws
- Knife or grinder to cut backer board
- Drill-driver
- Thinset mortar

1 A standard 2-ft.-wide counter made with 2x4s has a gap of about 17 in. between the front and back. A single layer of cement-based backer board is sufficiently strong to span that gap and support a tile top and a grill. To be safe, you may want to add a second layer. Or add 2x4 support braces laid flat and attached every 16 in. or so using angle-driven screws or nails as shown.

2 Cut and lay a sheet of backer board that will overhang the finished counter surface by an inch or more. Drive backer-board screws every 6 in. into the top plates and the cross braces.

3 If you will install tiles, determine the thickness of the edging. If you need to thicken the substrate, cut strips of backer board and attach them to the underside of the overhanging substrate. Butter the strip with thinset mortar. Hold the strip with your hand as you drive short screws to temporarily secure the pieces until the mortar sets. Then remove the screws.

Ceramic-Tile Countertop

Ceramic tile offers an inexpensive way to install a sturdy, washable countertop surface. The stone-look tiles shown on these pages have a natural, earthy appearance that never goes out of style. But you don't have to settle for a classic look: given the variety of tile colors and shapes available, it can be fun to personalize your outdoor kitchen with a one-of-a-kind countertop.

Outdoor tiles must be installed especially firmly because the weather takes its toll: it is not uncommon for a tiled top to come apart after a few seasons of use. If you choose the right materials and install them correctly, however, a tiled top can survive in extreme climates for many years.

- **Use tiles made for countertops or for floors.** Soft wall tiles can be colorful and attractive but will likely crack.
- **Install cross braces, and firmly attach backer-board substrate** so that it is rock solid. Even a slight amount of flex can cause tiles to pop loose.
- **Set the tiles in high-quality polymer-fortified thinset mortar, and make sure that the tiles are fully embedded at all points.** For even greater strength, you can use three-part epoxy resin mortar, though it is much more expensive.
- **Fill the joints with epoxy grout.** You will spend more time wiping it clean during installation, but it will reliably seal the joints and remain cleanable. Choose a color that matches or complements the tile; grout in a contrasting color may sound like a good idea, but it exaggerates minor imperfections and tends to produce an amateurish appearance.

The exposed edges of most ceramic tiles are unattractive. Purchase special edging and corner tiles so that all visible surfaces will be glazed. Here we show installing V-cap edging, but you may choose instead to install bullnose tiles around the perimeter and narrow edge tiles below the bullnose. Wood-trim edging is charming, but it is not a durable solution for an outdoor counter.

Snap Cutter

If you need to make only straight cuts rather than notches or cutouts, you can use a tile snap cutter on most ceramic tile (not stone tile). To cut a series of tiles all the same size, adjust and tighten the sliding guide. Place the tile against the guide; press the cutting wheel down onto the tile; and slide it across the tile in one motion to score the tile's surface. Position the pressure plate so that it pushes down on both sides of the score, and press down to snap the tile in two.

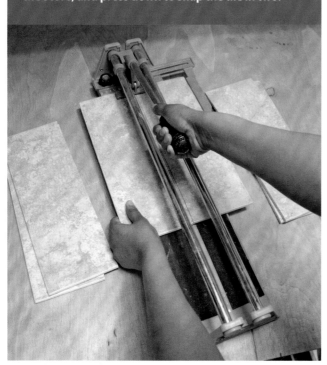

You can create a completely customized design using ceramic tiles. Here, diamond-shaped accents add pizzazz to a neutral palette and make the backsplash more interesting.

Installing a Ceramic-Tile Countertop

• Ceramic Tiles • V-Cap or other edging tiles • Thinset mortar • Epoxy grout • Masonry wet saw • Snap tile cutter • Square-notched trowel • Plastic spacers • Bucket and margin trowel • Sponge-type grout float • Grout sponge

1 If you are using V-cap edge tiles, slide one of them along the perimeter where they will be installed, and hold a pencil against it to draw a layout line for the field tiles.

2 Position some field tiles using plastic spacers to mimic the grout joints, and mark for any needed cuts. Marking for a sink opening from below is shown here.

3 Make the cuts using a tile wet saw, as shown here, or a snap cutter for straight cuts (opposite page). Rent or buy the saw, and follow instructions to keep the blade wet at all times while cutting.

4 Test-fit full-size tiles, cut tiles, and edge tiles. Use spacers to maintain consistent grout lines. Check that the grill, burner, or sink, or any combination, will fit into the opening(s).

Continued on next page

Installing a Ceramic-Tile Countertop, cont'd.

5 Mix a batch of fortified thinset mortar in a bucket, following the manufacturer's instructions. The mortar should be the consistency of mayonnaise, firm enough to stick to a trowel.

6 Use a square-notched trowel to spread and comb the mortar. Hold the trowel at a consistent angle, and scrape lightly on the backer board to produce a setting bed of even thickness.

9 Check the layout. Aim for straight, evenly spaced grout lines. If you get mortar on your hands or the tiles, wash or wipe it off immediately. Allow the mortar to set overnight or longer. Once the mortar sets, you can grout the joints.

10 Mix epoxy grout according to directions, and scoop it onto the surface, holding the grout float nearly flat as you press grout into the joints. Make sure that the joints are completely filled.

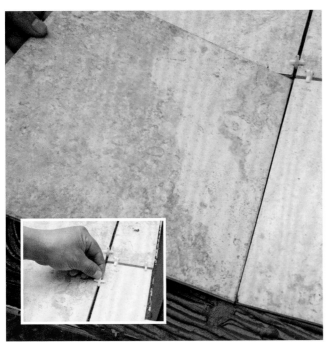

7 Lower the tiles into place. Do not slide them more than ½ in. or so. Use plastic spacers to maintain the joints (inset). Press down with your hand to bed the tile firmly in the mortar.

8 You may need to butter the edge tiles with mortar where they meet the edge of the backer board. You can adjust the position of the edge tiles in or out and up or down by adding or subtracting mortar.

11 Tip the float, and use it to scrape away excess grout before it starts to harden. Move the float diagonally so as not to dig into the joints. Use the float's wide edge for large sections and its front edge for smaller areas.

12 Fill a bucket with water; dampen a grout sponge; and wipe the surface. Rinse the sponge often, and use it to create joints of even heights. Allow the grout to harden; then buff the tiles using a dry cloth.

LEFT Handsome faux-stone tiles with a cooler, formal feel give this kitchen an ambiance that is reminiscent of an indoor kitchen.

BELOW A variety of natural materials gives this kitchen an eclectic feel. The tall backsplash provides privacy from neighbors and adds interest to the design.

Flagstone Countertops

The term "flagstone" generally refers to any large stone that is ¾–2 inches thick. The actual kind of stone varies; limestone and sandstone are two of the more common. Some flagstones have deep pits, while others are nearly flat. Some are irregularly formed; others are cut to geometric shapes.

If you don't mind a somewhat rough working surface, consider installing flagstones for the countertop. This can be an inexpensive option; it will basically have the same square-foot price as a flagstone patio.

Use a grinder equipped with a diamond blade to cut flagstones. For a more natural-looking appearance you may choose to tap the cut edge with a hammer or rough it up using a grinder (as shown for rough stone on page 166). You can allow the flagstones to overhang the counter by 1–2 inches, and the overhanging edge can be irregular in shape.

Set flagstones in a thick bed of standard masonry mortar (rather than thinset). Allow the mortar to dry; then use a grout bag to fill the joints with more mortar. (See pages 132–33 for using a grout bag.) Allow a few days for the mortar to cure; then protect the stones from staining with two or three coats of masonry sealer.

ABOVE The natural beauty of flagstone has an irresistible charm in an outdoor kitchen. Careful choosing and cutting will minimize unevenness.

BOTTOM LEFT The warm colors in these stones, combined with the taupe-colored stucco, make this counter fit naturally in a Southwestern landscape.

BELOW The gleaming grill at this kitchen's center is framed by thick, uneven stone in both the counter and counterop for a pleasant rustic effect.

Pour-in-Place Concrete Countertop

A concrete countertop can be remarkably inexpensive; all you really need is bags of concrete mix, some simple metal reinforcement, wood for temporary forms, and perhaps some colorant. Also, a top that is poured in place, right side up, is tricky but requires no special masonry skills.

The result is a top that may be variously described as "organic," "rustic," or even "shabby"; expect imperfections and perhaps trowel marks. It will, however, be smooth enough for countertop use. You will need to seal it every year or so using masonry sealer.

Artisan concrete tops are typically fabricated upside down in forms made of melamine. You can find companies online that will sell you special concrete mixes and tools, as well as detailed instructions, for creating a top that is a work of art. Building the top may become a sort of hobby for you. The materials are more expensive than the ones we show on the next six pages but still make for a reasonably priced countertop.

You can order bags of special countertop concrete, which is pretty certain not to crack and is easy to work with, from most home centers. It is made from white cement, which makes colors more vivid. You can also achieve good results using bags of *high-early-strength* concrete mix. Just be sure to make the mix as dry as possible. Add fiber reinforcement, which you can buy from a concrete supplier or from online sources, to improve crack resistance. The fibers will appear in the final surface, however, making it slightly less smooth.

To calculate how much concrete you need, go to a concrete supplier's Web site, and search for a countertop mix calculator. There you can enter the square footage and thickness of your top to learn how many bags to buy. When calculating the square footage, be sure to subtract for the grill, burners, sink, and any other gaps. Here is a simple calculator that covers many situations.

In the following pages we show a simple top, lightly colored and treated to expose the aggregate. You may choose to add decorative elements such as colored stones.

The project has a grill and burner that are inside the countertop. If an appliance will protrude beyond the front or back of the top, construct a substrate and form with a cutout that is the right size.

Mix a test batch of concrete, adding colorant. Calculate the amount of colorant you will need to maintain the same ratio in your real batch. Allow the test batch to cure for several days. If you do not like the color, experiment with concrete acid stains until you achieve a color that pleases you.

A concrete countertop can be an elegant choice for an outdoor kitchen. A flawlessly smooth surface like this may require assistance from professional fabricators.

SQUARE FEET (M²)	6 (0.56)	10 (0.93)	25 (2.32)
1.5" thick # of 80 lb. (36.3 kg) bags	2	3	6
2" thick # of 80 lb. (36.3 kg) bags	2	3	7

Pour-in-Place Concrete Countertop

- Concrete mix (countertop or high-early-strength) • 6-in. ladder-type masonry reinforcement • Concrete colorant
- 2x2s and 2x4s for forms • Caulk • Rigid foam insulation and duct tape (for making inner forms) • Wire cutters • Spray cooking oil
- Wheelbarrow or mason's tub • Hoe and shovel • Rubber gloves • Magnesium or wooden float • Concrete edging tool
- Steel trowel • Drill-driver, bits • Reciprocating saw • Random-orbit sander • Muriatic acid, baking soda• Acid stain for concrete

1 Install a backer-board substrate that comes flush to the outside of the counter. (See pages 126–27.) For a countertop that will overhang the counter by 1½ in., cut and attach lengths of 2x2 to the perimeter, flush with the top of the backer board.

2 Attach 2x4s to the 2x2s to create forms for the outside edges. Here, the 2×4s are screwed with their bottoms flush with the bottoms of the 2x2s, to make a form for a 2-in.-thick top. If you want a thinner top, bring the 2x4s down accordingly.

3 Apply caulk to the inside edges so that the form will be smooth and gap-free all around. Where needed, make inner forms for a burner or grill using the methods shown on pages 181–83.

4 Cut pieces of 6-in. masonry reinforcement to fit inside the formed area. It is made of No. 9 wire, which most experts agree is the right thickness for the purpose. The wire does not need to be cut precisely, as long as it will generally reinforce the concrete.

Continued on next page

Pour-in-Place Concrete Countertop, cont'd.

5 To keep the concrete from sticking to the wooden forms, spray them with cooking oil. Do not use form-release oil because it can discolor the concrete.

6 Pour about 2 in. of water into a wheelbarrow or mason's tub; then add a bag of concrete mix. Combine the colorant of your choice with additional water, and work the color into the concrete as you mix it.

9 Wearing rubber gloves, press the concrete firmly against the forms at all points. Tap the sides of the wooden forms with a hammer, and press again to remove air bubbles.

10 Use a length of 2x4 that is a foot or more longer than the width of the countertop forms to generally smooth the surface—a process called screeding. Employ a back-and-forth sawing motion as you move the screed board along the surface.

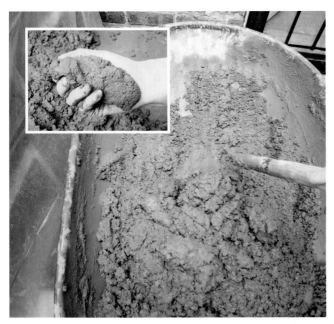

7 Mix the concrete thoroughly, adding only as much water as needed to get it completely wet. Aim for a firm mixture that you can roll into a ball with your hand (inset). Scrape the bottom and sides of the wheelbarrow or tub to be sure you have mixed all of the ingredients.

8 Remove the metal reinforcement, keeping track of where it goes. Use a shovel to place the concrete around and against the forms. Press the metal reinforcement into the concrete so that it is suspended halfway through the thickness of the top.

11 After screeding once, you will likely have a series of voids. Fill them with concrete as needed, and screed again.

12 Smooth the surface using a magnesium or wooden float. Where possible, span the float between forms. Elsewhere, use a light touch to maintain an even surface. Hold the float close to flat, and use long, sweeping strokes. Once surface water appears, stop and let it dry.

Continued on next page

Pour-in-Place Concrete Countertop, cont'd.

13 Use an edging tool to produce a rounded edge on the perimeter. Insert the edger's flange between the form board and the concrete, and run it back and forth several times until the edge surface is smooth.

14 Once the surface has no pools of water, gently smooth it using a steel trowel. You will probably not achieve professional results, but with care you can remove most of the obvious trowel marks. Avoid overworking; stop as soon as water reappears on the surface.

16 Wait a few hours for the top to get hard; then cover it loosely with plastic to keep it moist. (The slower the top cures, the stronger the concrete will be.) After a day or two, remove any other forms. If you have an inside form like this, drill holes at the corners, then use a reciprocating saw (inset) to cut out the backer board on the inside.

17 To expose some of the concrete's aggregate and create a stonier appearance, abrade the surface after a couple of days using a belt or random-orbit sander. Dampen the surface, and slowly sand it, starting with 30-grit wet/dry sandpaper. Repeat the process as necessary, moving on to successively higher grits, until you achieve the surface you desire.

15 Remove the screws from one of the 2x4s after an hour or so, and gently pull the board away. If the concrete holds its shape, pull all of the 2x4s out; if not, wait and try again later. Use an edger to smooth the now-exposed edge.

18 Once the top has completely cured—turning a lighter color when fully dry—protect it with stone or masonry sealer. Some sealers are meant to soak in, while others coat the surface; the best products do both. Apply the sealer using a clean rag; allow the sealer to dry; then reapply. Reapply sealer again every year or so or whenever rainwater appears to stop beading.

Acid to Expose Aggregate

Once the top has cured (become both hard and dry), you can use muriatic acid to expose aggregate. Mix one part acid with two parts water. (Always pour the acid into the water, NEVER the other way around.) Wearing nitrile gloves, protective eyewear, and long clothing, scrub the acid solution into the surface (below left). Wait a few minutes; sprinkle the surface with baking soda to halt the acidic reaction; and scrub again (below right). Rinse several times.

Acid Staining

If you want to darken the surface or change its color after the concrete has cured, apply acid stain. If possible, experiment on an inconspicuous spot first. Mix the stain with water, and apply it using a clean sponge. Repeat if you want a deeper color.

Counter with a Kamado Grill

With the growing popularity of kamado grills, many homeowners are choosing to incorporate them into an outdoor kitchen counter. See page 37 for tips on choosing a kamado grill.

As shown on pages 68 and 82, you can simply place a kamado grill on an open shelf, which is easy to build and shows off the whole grill. You can also purchase a rolling cart, perhaps with a small wooden counter on each side, and simply roll it up next to your counter. But if you build one into a countertop, it will appear more integrated, and you will find food preparation more convenient.

We show making a concrete countertop with a round opening, but you may choose to hire professionals to cut a granite slab to fit. You could use tile or flagstone for the countertop, but it would require painstakingly careful cutting.

Most of the steps for a kamado-surround counter are the same as for any other outdoor kitchen counter. (See pages 117–19, 126–27, and 134–38). The next four pages show some of the special methods for supporting a heavy grill that is round in shape. Here are some things to keep in mind:

■ If you buy a small kamado grill, it may fit into a standard 24-inch-wide counter, but **for a larger unit you will need to widen the counter.** Keep in mind the dimensions of the framing pieces as well as the thickness of the backer board and finish material.

■ **The kamado grill must rest on a solidly framed shelf.** This does not need to be elaborate, as Step 1 shows.

■ **Refer to manufacturer's specifications,** and carefully plan how tall the shelf needs to be so that the kamado unit will be at the correct height and you will be able to raise and lower the lid. Take into account the total thickness of the countertop.

■ **Be sure to provide ample access below the grill** for ash removal and the lower vent control. With some models, you may need to provide access for a chip feeder as well. You may choose to simply leave a large opening for these (as we show in the following steps), or you can build an access door.

BELOW This counter, with its kamado grill and burner, offers cooking flexibility and keeps all of the mess outside. You will need an access hole as shown to remove the kamado's ashes.

Counter with a Kamado Grill

1 Frame the counter using wood or metal studs, being sure to allow enough space between the top plates for the kamado grill. To support the shelf at the correct height, frame an opening in the front, and add a cleat at the back. Check that they are level with each other and 1½ in. below the finished height of the shelf.

2 If the shelf will be visible, make it out of cedar heartwood (as shown here) or some other good-looking and rot-resistant wood. Also install trim pieces at the sides. Have the shelf and trim pieces protrude past the backer board by at least 1½ in. so that you can butt the finish material up against them (as shown on page 136).

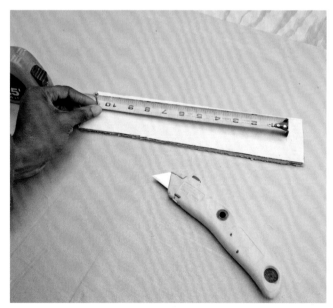

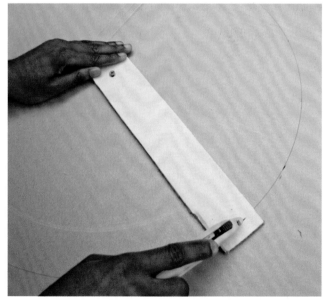

3 We made a circular form using rigid foam insulation (here, two thicknesses of 1-in. boards). Consult the manufacturer's literature to find out the size of the hole you need. Make a simple trammel out of a piece of cardboard. Make a mark near the end, and poke in a screw at the radius dimension (half the diameter), piercing the insulation.

4 Poke a sharp (new) knife blade straight down through the mark, and hold it straight upright as you slide the trammel around to cut a circle. Make the first pass about ½ in. deep; then cut again to complete the cut. Measure to be sure that the circle is the right diameter; if not, try again.

Continued on next page

Counter with a Kamado Grill, cont'd.

5 Cut another circle. Apply caulk to the top of the bottom piece, and duct-tape the two pieces together. Tape the perimeter; then add short pieces of tape to the top. Smooth the tape firmly so it will stay in place when you trowel the concrete (Step 7). The form does not need to be perfect, but the top piece should be cleanly round.

6 Attach the countertop backer-board substrate, and build the form for the concrete. (See page 175). Determine where you want the kamado grill to go; apply beads of caulk; and set the form in the caulk. Measure to double-check the form's location, and allow at least an hour for the caulk to set.

9 Use a framing square to check that the bottom of the concrete will not butt against the grill. Sand away any protrusions using a belt sander equipped with a 60-grit sanding belt. Also use the belt sander or a random-orbit sander to slightly round over the top edge of the hole so that there are no sharp edges.

10 Lighten the grill by removing its top. In most cases, you remove the screws holding the strap, rather than disconnecting the hinge. Position the grill's feet (if any) on the shelf. Working with a helper or two, carefully lower the grill into position. If the fit is too tight, perhaps set tiles on the shelf to raise the grill a bit.

7 Mix the concrete; shovel it onto the countertop; screed it; and trowel it, as shown on pages 176–79. Push the concrete up against the form, but there is no need to tool the edge as with the countertop outer edges. After the concrete has hardened enough to remove the wooden form, wait at least an hour and perhaps a day to remove the circular form.

8 Use a flat pry bar or a scraper to cut and pry out the form. There is no need to fill in the gaps around the perimeter because they will not show once the grill is in place. Use a masonry bit to drill a starter hole or two (inset); then cut the backer board using a reciprocating saw equipped with a masonry blade.

11 The countertop will typically come within about ⅛ in. of the grill all around. Apply sealer to the concrete. During heavy rains, water will drip down to the shelf below, so keep the shelf well sealed as well.

Cooking with a Kamado

Even when a kamado grill gets up into the 700-degree-F range, it is not uncomfortable to work near the unit because it encases the heat so efficiently. For extra flavor, use the tool provided to add hardwood chips (inset).

Pizza Oven

Several companies sell pizza-oven kits that can be shipped to your home. The ones shown here are designed and fabricated by Sergio De Paula for his company Fogazzo Wood-Fired Ovens & Barbecues. This type of oven does not require a roof and can be installed on top of a structure made with metal studs and backer board. It is a "treasure chest" shape—rectangular, with an arched top. (Some ovens are round in shape, but De Paula has found that a rounded top is all that is needed to maintain even temperatures throughout the oven and avoid burning the pizza or bread.)

The instructions here are general. Consult with the manufacturer to learn all of the steps you need to support and install an oven. Purchase a chimney tall enough to carry smoke away from any nearby buildings.

BELOW AND RIGHT The finished oven may have a single large space at the bottom (below), or you may choose to divide it into two compartments (right). You also may want to wrap the opening with decorative tile.

Pizza Oven

1 Build a metal-stud frame about 4 ft. tall to support the oven and provide storage space below for the firewood. (See pages 120–23.) At its top, the frame should have bracing every 12 in. or so, topped by a layer of backer board. Set the fireplace's concrete floor base on top of the framing. (This one uses two layers.)

2 Position the oven's threshold on the base (inset), and add firebricks to complete the floor. You would typically lay the firebricks dry, but it is OK to lay them in a bed of refractory mortar if you prefer.

3 Set the kit on top of the base. This model has a concrete chamber with a decorative door surround. (Here, the builder has chosen to use gypsum-based exterior sheathing boards instead of cement-based backer board for the counter surround.)

4 Install the chimney. Use metal framing to create a seamless wall running up from the structure below and around the oven. This provides several inches of room for insulation. Attach stucco lath to the framing. (See page 135.) Then fill the space between the lath and the oven with vermiculite, and apply stucco as shown on pages 136–38.

Building an Eating Counter

If an eating counter—which is typically 42 inches or so high—is attached to a wide counter below, it usually needs only some large brackets (or corbels) to keep it in place. (See, for example, page 128.) A narrow eating counter like the one shown below, however, requires a bit of engineering to keep it standing sturdily upright. (We describe this counter on page 92.) In this case, the builders anchored the counter's frame to the deck's framing and then installed support pillars, clad in PVC sheeting, on each side.

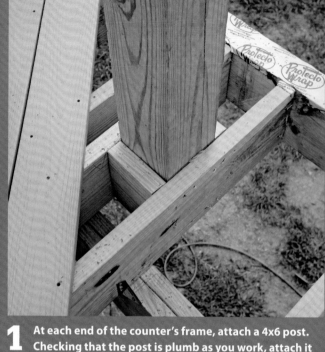

1 At each end of the counter's frame, attach a 4x6 post. Checking that the post is plumb as you work, attach it to one of the joists. Then install short framing pieces along all four sides of the post; they should fit snugly. Drive lots of screws or nails.

4 Build simple pillars out of 2x6s, two in the front and three in the back. Anchor the pillar frames by driving screws into the studs. Enlist some strong help, and rest the granite pieces on top of the pillars.

2 Install the decking; then build a simple 2x6 stud frame between the posts. Make sure that the studs are no farther apart than 16 in. on center.

3 Wrap the frame with cement-based backer board. Make sure that the top piece is level because the top piece of granite rests on it; you may need to use a rasp (as shown here) to provide a perfectly flat surface.

5 Check that the granite pieces are level in both directions, and slip in shims as needed. Tilt the counter pieces up; apply a thick bead of silicone caulk; then reset the counters. Do the same for the backsplash piece (inset).

6 Wrap the pillars with PVC sheeting or another finish of your choice. Attach the PVC using silicone caulk and finishing nails. Now you are ready to apply the finish to the areas between the pillars. (See pages 128–33 for applying faux stone.)

Churrasco Grill

You can purchase a churrasco grill in kit form; the following instructions generally show how to put one together and finish it. The basic parts are made of refractory concrete and firebrick. You will finish the insides and fascia with tiles that are heat resistant and cover the sides with stucco, tiles, or veneer stones or bricks.

The kit is heavy, so it should rest on a concrete pad at least 4 inches thick; there is no need for a thick footing. Most kits come with a short chimney, so position it at least 12 feet away from a house or other structure so that smoke has ample room to escape.

Buy a rotisserie unit made to fit into the churrasco. Some rotisseries are motorized; other less-expensive ones are manual.

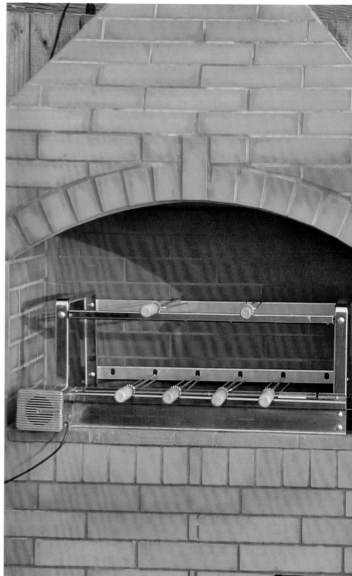

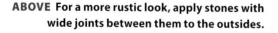

ABOVE For a more rustic look, apply stones with wide joints between them to the outsides.

TOP RIGHT In this example the homeowner used the same tiles for the sides as for the insides. Set the outside tiles in standard thinset mortar, and set the tiles inside the firebox using refractory mortar. Apply grout to the outside tiles, and use refractory mortar to fill the joints inside.

RIGHT A motorized or hand-crank churrasco rotisserie turns all of the spits at the same time.

Churrasco Grill

• Churrasco kit • Type-N mortar • Hammer drill and bits • Refractory mortar • Tiles for the inside and the opening • Finish material for the sides • Rotisserie to fit

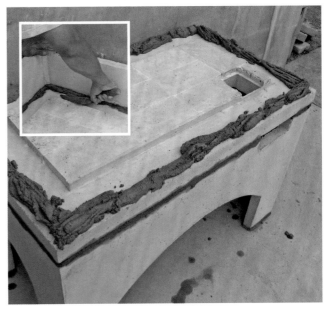

1 Uncrate the kit (inset), and inspect all of the parts. Mix a batch of Type-N mortar, and set the legs of the base in beds of the mortar. Check that the base is level, adding or subtracting mortar as necessary to make it so. Drill holes, and attach an anchor to each of the legs.

2 Assemble the parts in order, setting each in a bed of mortar. At the bottom of the grill opening, set firebricks for a floor. Set the next piece in place, and trowel refractory mortar all around the firebricks (inset).

3 Once you have assembled the concrete unit (inset), apply the finish materials. If you choose to tile the firebox and stucco the outsides, first apply heat-resistant tiles. Fill the joints with refractory mortar.

4 Protect the tiles with tape and construction paper. Apply stucco lath and corner bead. (See page 135.) Attach the lath by drilling holes and driving short masonry screws with washers (inset). Apply the stucco in two coats, keeping each coat moist so that it dries slowly. (See pages 136–38.)

Installing a Sink

Installing a sink or sinks is a fairly straightforward job once you have run the supply and drain lines into the counter. (See pages 112–15.) A small bar-type sink about 15 inches square is a common choice. But you can install a larger one if you plan to do a lot of food preparation and cleaning. See pages 74–75 for tips on choosing a sink. Many sinks come packaged with the faucet and basket strainer; if not, buy them separately.

If you install a self-rimming sink as shown on these pages, you do not have to cut the countertop hole precisely. For an under-mounted sink, on the other hand, you must make a clean, accurate cut in the countertop and finish the exposed edges. Most often, this means hiring a granite company to cut the hole for you. They can supply the hardware needed for mounting the sink, or they may mount the sink for you.

You could mount the sink onto the counter and then install the plumbing, but it is much easier to install as much plumbing as possible ahead of time.

ABOVE A drop-in beverage unit like this is not difficult to install, as long as the opening is correctly sized and the basic plumbing is in place.

RIGHT This fairly large one-bowl sink is equipped with a faucet, which has a pull-out spout/sprayer, as well as a soap dispenser.

Installing a Sink

- Stainless-steel self-rimming sink • Faucet (which may
- Supply tubes to reach the stop valves • Adjustable wrench

1 Mount the faucet onto the sink. For a two-handle model, slip the gasket onto the faucet body; thread the two inlets through the hole; and fasten the faucet with two gaskets and nuts, as shown. If you have a one-handle faucet, you will thread all of the plumbing through the single hole and then attach it using a mounting ring and a nut.

come with the sink) • **Basket strainer** • **Plumber's putty** • **Spud wrench to tighten the strainer**
• **PVC P-trap** • **Mounting clips** • **Caulk and gun** • **Screwdriver**

2 Install a basket strainer in the sink's hole (top). Apply a ring of plumber's putty around the hole on the inside of the sink; slip on the gaskets; and tighten the nut on the underside. Fasten flexible supply tubes to the faucet inlets (bottom). Make sure the tubes are long enough to reach the stop valves inside the cabinet and that they fit the valves.

3 Assemble a P-trap (which comes in a kit), and fasten it to the basket strainer. Be sure that all of the washers are in place, and tighten the nuts. (This kind of nut tightens by hand.) Test to see that the drain will reach the trap adapter inside the counter. You may need to cut one or two pieces or add an extension piece.

4 Slip the mounting clips into the sink's channels. There should be at least two flanges on each side. Turn or flip up the flanges so that they can fit into the hole. Apply a bead of caulk or plumber's putty to the underside of the flange. Position the sink, and make sure the caulk or putty seals all around. From below, tighten the mounting clips (inset).

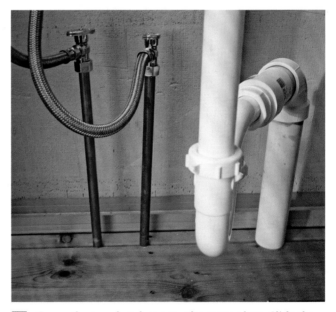

5 Screw the supply tubes onto the stop valves. Slide the P-trap's arm into the trap adapter (the elbow on top of the drainpipe at the back of the cabinet), and tighten the nuts. Turn on the water, and test for leaks.

191

Installing Grills and Burners

The last step in an outdoor kitchen project is usually
sliding in the grill, burners, and other appliances.
As long as you made openings of the correct size as
described in manufacturer's instructions, this is should
be straightforward. Be sure that the grill or burner is
suited to your gas source—either natural gas, which
comes from your house through a pipe, or propane (LP),
which connects to a tank inside the counter.

Follow the manufacturer's installation instructions.
You install most grills by simply sliding or dropping the
unit into place. Other grills require first installing a metal
sleeve for heat protection. Most gas grills are not too
heavy, so two people can easily carry and install them.
If you have a giant 48-inch-wide unit, you may need a
third person. If you are incorporating a cart grill into
your island, see page 69.

**Offering instant heat, a simple side burner may lure your
family outside more often.**

Anchoring a Drop-In Burner

Some side burners slide in like a grill. Many drop-in
units do not have fastening hardware. You could just let
it sit there, but it may move while you cook. To anchor
it, first draw its outline on the countertop (right). (Slide
the unit slightly over after drawing the first two lines
so that the lines will not be visible when you install the
burner.) Apply a fairly thick bead of clear silicone along
the lines (below), and set the burner into it. Scrape away
the excess (bottom right); then clean with a solvent-
dampened rag. Allow a day for the silicone to fully set.

Grill Installation

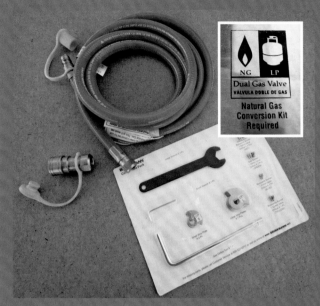

Consult with your dealer to get the flexible line hookups you need. If your gas grill has a "dual gas valve" label (inset), for example, you will need a conversion kit like this in order to hook it to a propane kit.

Attach the flexible gas line to the underside of the grill or burner you want to install. Check that its other end will reach the gas line or propane tank. Also check that the connection will fit at the pipe or tank. If there is a connection problem, take as many parts as possible to a plumbing supplier to get the right parts.

To install a grill, slowly slide it in, taking care not to bump against the grill's siding or bend the gas connections attached to the grill. Once you are certain of the fit, you may choose to lift it up slightly and apply silicone caulk under the flanges to make a watertight seal. If there is no flange on the back (as with this grill), simply apply a bead of caulk there.

Once you have installed the grill, there may be a gap like this between the grill and the counter in the front. This is normal and prevents overheating of the grill and counter.

Index

Resource Guide

The following list of manufacturers and associations is meant to be a general guide to additional industry and product-related sources. It is not intended as a complete listing of products and manufacturers represented in this book.

Alfresco Open Air Culinary Systems
Commerce, CA
www.alfrescogrills.com; (888) 383-8800
Manufacturer of a complete line of restaurant-inspired luxury outdoor kitchen appliances, including grills, side burners, power burners, refrigerators, prep sinks, beverage centers, plating and garnish centers, wood and gas-fired pizza ovens, and a host of accessories to create a fully functional outdoor kitchen.

Allan Block Corp.
Bloomington, MN
www.allanblock.com; (952) 835-5309
Installation of environmentally friendly mortarless wall systems, such as stackable blocks for retaining walls and residential landscaping, as well as lights, grill surrounds, privacy fences, and more.

Ancient Art of Stone
Victoria, BC, Canada
www.ancientartofstone.com; (250) 886-1612
Design and fabrication of functional art forms for private and public venues in the medium of stone, often from the mountains and valleys of Vancouver Island.

Atlantis Outdoor Kitchens
(Division of Custom Wood Products, LLC)
Roanoke, VA
www.outdoorkitchensbyatlantis.com; (877) 223-4537
Manufacturer of custom weatherproof outdoor cabinets, supplier of design services and outdoor appliances.

Barrett Outdoors
Millstone Township, NJ
www.barrettoutdoors.com; (866) 418-1891
Builder of custom decks, shade structures, outdoor kitchens, and patios.

Blue Sky Building Company
Shallotte, NC
www.blueskybuildingcompany.com; (910) 755-3444
Custom home builders and renovators.

Breckenridge Landscape
New Berlin, WI
www.Breckenridgelandscape.com; (262) 364-1719
Complete landscape design and installation services, including 3D modeling, planting designs, elevations, perspectives, color rendering, fly-through videos, and even designs for the do-it-yourselfer.

Bull Outdoor Products
Rialto, CA
www.bullbbq.com; (800) 521-2855
Manufacturer of quality grill products, including grill islands, fire features, grilling accessories ranging from tools and starters to sauces and rubs, and outdoor kitchen components like doors, sinks, warming drawers, sound systems, and vent hoods.

Cal Flame (Division of LMS, Inc.)
Pomona, CA
www.calflamebbq.com; (909) 623-8781 or (800) 225-7727
Hearth and barbecue manufacturer that offers innovative backyard products for every home and budget, including BBQ grills, grilling and drop-in accessories, customized BBQ outdoor kitchens, BBQ islands, custom BBQ carts, fireplaces, and fire pits.

Char-Broil (Division of W.C. Bradley Co.)
Columbus, GA
www.charbroil.com; (866) 239-6777
Manufacturer of quality outdoor cooking products, including grills, smokers and fryers, and grilling accessories, and a leading name in infrared technology.

Chicago Brick Oven

Elmhurst, IL

www.chicagobrickoven.com; (630) 359-4793

Leading U.S. manufacturer of brick ovens for outdoor kitchens and outdoor entertaining.

Cipriano Landscape Design

Mahwah, NJ

www.PlantNJ.com; (201) 785-0800

Design and installation of luxury outdoor living areas, including outdoor dining areas, outdoor fireplaces, outdoor living rooms, and luxurious fire pits featuring custom stonework.

Coastroad Hearth & Patio Supply Co.

Shallotte, NC

www.coastroadonline.com; (910) 755-7611

Supplier and installer of an array of products for hearth and patio living spaces, including fireplaces, fire pits, grills, cabinetry, access doors and drawers, and a range of amenities such as refrigerators, umbrellas, sinks, warming drawers, and more.

Crimson Valley Landscaping

Rockford, IL

www.crimsonvalleylandscaping.com; (815) 397-1860

Landscape design and construction, offering a full range of options for the backyard, including designing and building outdoor kitchens, bars, fireplaces, fire pits, patios, decks, walkways, overheads, retaining walls, seating, lighting, irrigation, water features, fences, and gates.

D&M Outdoor Living

Western Springs, IL

www.dmoutdoorliving.com; (630) 654-8400

Hardscape and landscape designer and installer of outdoor kitchens, grill stations, decks, patios, walkways, fireplaces, fire pits, arbors, pergolas, and hot tubs using wood, composite materials, and stone.

Dal-Tile Corp. (Division of Mohawk Industries)
Dallas, TX
www.daltile.com; (214) 398-1411
Manufacturer of ceramic tile and natural stone products, including glazed and unglazed tile, glazed and unglazed ceramic mosaics, glazed porcelain tile, unglazed quarry tile, and a variety of stone products.

Danver Stainless Steel Cabinetry
Wallingford, CT
www.danver.com; (888) 441-0537
Outdoor lifestyle products, including cabinets, grills, refrigeration units, sinks, faucets, and overheads.

DCS by Fisher & Paykel Appliances
Huntington Beach, CA
www.dcsappliances.com; (888) 936-7872
Manufacturer of commercial-quality outdoor cooktops and grills, as well as indoor professional-style products.

Decks by Kiefer
North Plainfield, NJ
www.decksbykiefer.com; (908) 303-6050
High-quality custom-deck builder.

Fine Decks, Inc.
Calvert County, MD
www.finedecks.com; (410) 286-9092
Designer and builder recognized as a national builder of the month in a professional deck builders magazine.

Fogazzo Wood Fired Ovens & BBQs
Arcadia, CA
www.fogazzo.com; (866) 364-2996
Manufacturer of wood-fired ovens, including a new line of ovens with a "treasure chest" shape and available as a kit, mesquite-fired churrasco Brazilian barbecues, and an extensive line of oven and barbecue accessories.

Huettl Landscape Architecture
Walnut Creek, CA

www.huettldesign.com; (925) 937-6400
Landscape design and construction company that strives for innovation and sustainability in design, creating comfortable and compelling outdoor living spaces that respond to the site, region, and needs of the client.

Integration Design Studio
Carlsbad, CA
www.integration-design.com; (760) 602-0144
Landscape architects for both residential and larger-scale community projects, including new custom home installation/construction, renovation, and water-wise gardens.

Inter IKEA Systems B.V.
Elizabeth, NJ
www.ikea.com/us; (888) 434-4532
Swedish-based international retailer that offers home furnishings for life improvement, emphasizing good design, function, and quality at low prices so that the majority of people can afford them.

JMC Designs LLC
Sugar Land, TX
www.jmcdesigns.biz; (832) 725-5133
Professional design firm specializing in new home construction and remodel design work.

Kalamazoo Outdoor Gourmet
Chicago, IL
www.KalamazooGourmet.com; (800) 868-1699
Manufacturer of outdoor kitchen equipment, including Hybrid Fire Grills—gas grills that also burn wood and charcoal—artisan pizza ovens that cook a thin-crust pie in three minutes, a wide range of outdoor refrigeration units, outdoor dishwashers, and stylish weather-tight outdoor cabinetry.

Legacy Design-Build
Becker, MN
www.legacydesign-build.com; (763) 856-9210
Builder specializing in new custom designed homes, whole house renovation, and home additions.

Lloyd/Flanders, Inc.
Menominee, MI
www.lloydflanders.com; (906) 863-4491
Manufacturer of fine woven outdoor furniture featuring beautiful design, master craftsmanship, and life-long durability.

Long Island Decking
Freeport, NY
www.lidecking.com; (516) 594-0390 or (631) 728-7272
Design and construction of decks, with an array of options, including outdoor kitchens, lighting, fences, awnings, pergolas, arbors, gazebos, patio pavers, and maintenance assistance.

Luxapatio
Miami, FL
www.luxapatio.com; (305) 477-5141
Specializing in outdoor designs for comfortable and luxurious spaces, including outdoor kitchens and equipment, pergolas, decks, pavers, artificial grass, and outdoor furniture.

Majestic Grill Parts
Sunrise, FL
www.grill-repair.com; (888) 346-6930
Supplier of gas barbecue grills, fireplaces, and outdoor furniture, as well as repair and service of gas barbecue grills.

Outdoor Creations
Phoenix, AZ
www.outdoorcreations.net; (520) 780-1645 or (480) 332-1962
Concrete and concrete-coating services, including decorative concrete, epoxy coatings, vertical decorative concrete, and construction of custom barbecues, fireplaces, and fire pits.

The Outdoor GreatRoom Co.
Eagan, MN
www.outdoorrooms.com; (866) 303-4028
Designer, manufacturer, and seller of pergolas, outdoor kitchens, grills, luxury outdoor furniture, fireplaces, fire pits, lighting, and heating products.

Outdoor Kitchens By Design, Inc.
Orange Park, FL
www.outdoorkitchensbydesign.com; (904) 264-2270
Designer and builder complete backyard designs, including custom outdoor kitchens, outdoor fireplaces, and courtyards, servicing Florida, Georgia, Tennessee, Missouri, and most of the Midwest.

Outdoor Living Made Easy
Northport, NY
www.olme.com; (631) 239-6480
Designer and builder of beautiful and functional outdoor kitchens, providing appliances, doors, drawers, patio furniture, gas grills and accessories, retractable awnings, waterproof sound systems, smokers, pizza ovens, umbrellas, and more.

Pedersen Associates, Landscape Architecture
San Rafael, CA
www.pedersenassociates.com; (415) 456-2070
Land planning and landscape architecture, creating environmentally sensitive designs for a natural flow between indoor and outdoor living areas.

Premier Grilling
Frisco, TX
www.premiergrilling.com; (855) 744-7455
Designer and builder of beautiful, functional backyards, supplying everything homeowners need for an outdoor kitchen, including patio furniture and a range of hearth and fireplace products.

R. H. Peterson Co.
City of Industry, CA
www.rhpeterson.com; (800) 332-3973
Manufacturer of high-quality grills, fire pits, and gas fireplace logs; brands include Fire Magic, American Outdoor Grills (AOG), Realfyre, and American Fyre Designs.

Rolling Ridge Deck and Outdoor Living Co., Inc.
Evergreen, CO
www.rollingridgedeck.com; (303) 670-4919

Designer and builder of custom decks, sunrooms, and outdoor living rooms in the Denver metropolitan area.

Saffire Grill Co.
Rockford, IL
www.saffiregrills.com; (815) 967-4100
Manufacturer of kamado-style charcoal-fired ceramic grill and smoker.

Signature Decks
Maumee, Ohio
www.sigdecks.com; (419) 277-5464
Custom deck builder specializing in outdoor living, with project options that include backyard decks, pergolas, fire pits, outdoor kitchens, built-in hot tubs, and outdoor lighting.

Stone Acorn Builders, LP
Bellaire, TX
www.stoneacorn.com; (713) 838-8808
Family-owned and -operated home-construction company that has been building quality houses since 1999 in the Houston area; member of *Southern Living* magazine's Custom Builder Program.

Stout Landscape Design Build
Los Angeles, CA
www.stoutdesignbuild.com; (310) 876-1018
Full-service design-and-build firm, LEED (Leadership in Energy and Environmental Design) certified by the U.S. Green Building Council for custom construction of residential homes and outdoor spaces.

Sub-Zero, Inc., and Wolf Appliance, Inc.
Madison, WI
www.subzero-wolf.com; (800) 222-7820
Manufacturer of food preservation and "anywhere" refrigeration, including built-in, under-counter, and integrated products for both indoor and outdoor kitchens under the Sub-Zero brand name; also manufacturer of a complete line of quality indoor and outdoor cooking products, including grills and warming drawers, under the Wolf brand name.

Sur La Table, Inc.
Seattle, WA
www.surlatable.com; (800) 243-0852
Retailer of quality cooking tools and accessories, from bakeware to cutlery to the hard-to-find.

Twin Eagles, Inc.
Cerritos, CA
www.twineaglesinc.com; (800) 789-2206
Manufacturer of built-in and freestanding grills and accessories, built-in burners and warming drawers, access doors and drawers, built-in bar accessories, gas and electric heaters, and ventilation equipment.

Unilock
Toronto, ON, Canada
www.unilock.com; (800) UNILOCK (864-5625)
Manufacturer of concrete and stone-look paver and stacking blocks for homeowners to create a unique outdoor living space.

Unique Deck Builders Inc.
Highland Park, IL
www.uniquedeck.com; (847) 831-1388
Designer and builder of unique decks and outdoor environments, plus deck cleaning, staining, and repairs.

Urrutia Design
Sausalito, CA
www.urrutiadesign.com; (415) 332-7777
Designer and remodeler of residential homes, focusing on major renovation of homes built in the nineteenth, twentieth, and twenty-first centuries in a variety of architectural styles.

Wayray Contracting, Inc.
Frisco, TX
www.wayraycontracting.com; (972) 712-7696
Contractor that aims to provide customers with an exceptional outdoor living area customized to their specific needs, using stone and wood to complement natural surroundings.

Credits

All photographs by Steve Cory and Diane Slavik except where noted.

page 1: courtesy of Sub-Zero/Wolf **page 2:** courtesy of Majestic Grill Parts **page 6:** courtesy of Sur la Table, Inc. **page 7:** courtesy of Danver Stainless Steel Cabinetry **page 8:** courtesy of Majestic Grill Parts **page 9:** courtesy of Blue Sky Building Co. **pages 10–11:** courtesy of Alfresco Open Air Culinary Systems **page 12:** courtesy of Luxapatio **page 13:** *top* courtesy of Atlantis Outdoor Kitchens; *bottom left* courtesy of Allan Block Corp.; *bottom right* Barbara Ries, designed by Pete Pedersen, Landscape Architect **page 14:** *left* courtesy of Sub-Zero/Wolf; *right* courtesy of Huettl Landscape Architecture **page 15:** *top* courtesy of Luxapatio; *bottom* courtesy of Rolling Ridge Deck and Outdoor Living Co., Inc. **page 16:** *top* courtesy of Justus Lambros, Signature Decks; *bottom left* courtesy of Rolling Ridge Deck and Outdoor Living Co., Inc.; *bottom right* courtesy of Integration Design Studio **page 17:** *top left* courtesy of Dal-Tile Corp.; *top right* courtesy of Dal-Tile Corp.; *bottom* courtesy of The Outdoor GreatRoom Co. **page 18:** *top left* courtesy of Cipriano Landscape Design; *bottom left* courtesy of Outdoor Living Made Easy; *bottom right* courtesy of Rolling Ridge Deck and Outdoor Living Co., Inc. **page 19:** courtesy of Majestic Grill Parts **page 20:** *top* courtesy of Stout Landscaping Design Build; *bottom* courtesy of Cipriano Landscape Design **page 21:** *top* courtesy of Crimson Valley Landscaping; *bottom left* courtesy of Majestic Grill Parts; *bottom right* courtesy of Stout Landscaping Design Build **page 22:** courtesy of Sub-Zero/Wolf **page 23:** *top left* courtesy of Outdoor Creations; *center* courtesy of Sub-Zero/Wolf; *bottom* courtesy of Cal Flame/Cal Spas **page 24:** *left* courtesy of IKEA; *right* Clemens Jellema, Fine Decks, Inc. **page 25:** *top left* courtesy of Integration Design Studio; *top right* and *bottom* courtesy of Urrutia Design; *center* courtesy of Wayray Contracting, Inc. **page 26:** *top left*

courtesy of Outdoor Kitchens By Design, Inc., designed by Mark Allen; *top right* courtesy of Cipriano Landscape Design; *bottom* courtesy of Coastroad Hearth & Patio Supply Co. **page 27:** courtesy of Outdoor Kitchens By Design, Inc., designed by Mark Allen **page 28:** Robin Cox; designed by JMC Designs and built by Collinas Design and Construction **page 29:** courtesy of Danver Stainless Steel Cabinetry **page 30:** courtesy of Outdoor Living Made Easy **page 31:** *top left* courtesy of IKEA; *top right* Barbara Ries, designed by Pete Pedersen, Landscape Architect; *bottom left* courtesy of Lloyd/Flanders, Inc.; *bottom right* courtesy of Stout Landscape Design Build **page 32:** *top* Jay Oliver, Long Island Decking; *center* courtesy of Danver Stainless Steel Cabinetry; *bottom* courtesy of Outdoor Kitchens By Design, Inc., deisgned by Mark Allen **page 33:** *top* courtesy of Luxapatio; *bottom* Joel Boyer, Unique Deck Builders, Inc. **page 34:** *left* courtesy of Premier Grilling; *right* courtesy of Kalamazoo Outdoor Gourmet **page 35:** Joel Boyer, Unique Deck Builders, Inc. **page 36:** *top* courtesy of DCS by Fisher & Paykel Appliances; *bottom* courtesy of Char-Broil; **page 37:** *top right* courtesy of Cal Flame/Cal Spas; *bottom* courtesy of Danver Stainless Steel Cabinetry **page 38:** *top* courtesy of The Outdoor GreatRoom Co.; *bottom left* courtesy of Outdoor Living Made Easy; *bottom right* courtesy of DCS by Fisher & Paykel Appliances **page 39:** *top* courtesy of Kalamazoo Outdoor Gourmet; *bottom* courtesy of Crimson Valley Landscaping **page 40:** Sergio de Paula, Fogazzo Wood Fired Ovens and Barbecues **page 41:** courtesy of Chicago Brick Oven **page 42:** *left* and *right* courtesy of The Outdoor GreatRoom Company **page 43:** *top* courtesy of DCS by Fisher & Paykel Appliances; *bottom* courtesy of Stout Landscape Design Build **page 44:** *top* courtesy of Lloyd/Flanders, Inc.; *bottom* courtesy of Outdoor Living Made Easy **page 45:** *top* and *bottom left* courtesy of Lloyd/Flanders, Inc.; *top right* courtesy of Luxapatio **page**

46: courtesy of Stout Landscape Design Build **page 47:** *top left* Clemens Jellema, Fine Decks, Inc.; *top right* courtesy of Outdoor Kitchens By Design, Inc., designed by Mark Allen; *bottom left* courtesy of The Outdoor GreatRoom Company; *bottom right* courtesy of Kalamazoo Outdoor Gourmet **pages 48–49:** courtesy of Cipriano Landscape Design **page 50:** courtesy of Stout Landscape Design Build **page 51:** *top left* courtesy of Danver Stainless Steel Cabinetry; *top right* courtesy of Outdoor Kitchens By Design, Inc., deisgned by Mark Allen; *bottom* courtesy of Coastroad Hearth & Patio Supply Co. **page 54:** *top* courtesy of Outdoor Living Made Easy; *center* courtesy of Wayray Contracting, Inc.; *bottom* courtesy of Majestic Grill Parts **page 55:** *top* courtesy of Stout Landscape Design Build; *center* courtesy of Cipriano Landscape Design; *bottom* courtesy of Outdoor Living Made Easy **page 56:** *top* courtesy of Outdoor Creations; *bottom* courtesy of Ancient Art of Stone; **page 57:** *top right* courtesy of Rolling Ridge Deck and Outdoor Living Co., Inc.; *bottom* courtesy of Premier Grilling; **page 58:** *top left* courtesy of Justus Lambros, Signature Decks; *bottom left* courtesy of Outdoor Living Made Easy **page 59:** courtesy of Danver Stainless Steel Cabinetry **page 61:** *center* courtesy of Bull Outdoor Products; *bottom left* courtesy of Stout Landscape Design Build; *bottom right* courtesy of Luxapatio **page 62:** *top left* courtesy of Crimson Valley Landscaping; *bottom left* Sergio de Paula, Fogazzo Wood Fired Ovens and Barbecues; *bottom right* courtesy of Stout Landscape Design Build **page 63:** *top left* courtesy of Luxapatio; *top right* Robin Cox, designed by JMC Designs and built by Collinas Design and Construction; *bottom* courtesy of Outdoor Kitchens By Design, Inc., designed by Mark Allen **page 64:** *top* courtesy of Outdoor Living Made Easy; *bottom left* courtesy of Cipriano Landscape Design; *bottom right* courtesy of Urrutia Design **page 65:** courtesy of Stout Landscape Design Build **page 66:** *center* courtesy of Outdoor Kitchens By Design, Inc., designed by Mark Allen; *bottom left* courtesy of Alfresco Open Air Culinary Systems; *bottom right* courtesy of Sub-Zero/Wolf **page 67:** courtesy of Outdoor Kitchens By Design, Inc., designed by Mark Allen **page 68:** courtesy of Majestic Grill Parts **page 69:** *bottom right* courtesy of Crimson Valley Landscaping **page 70:** *top left* courtesy of Sub-Zero/Wolf; *top right* courtesy of Alfresco Open Air Culinary Systems; *bottom* and **page 71:** courtesy of Twin Eagles BBQ Grill **page 72:** *top left* courtesy of Alfresco Open Air Culinary Systems; *top center* courtesy of Bull Outdoor Products; *top right* courtesy of Sub-Zero/Wolf; *bottom* courtesy of Twin Eagles BBQ Grill **page 73:** courtesy of Alfresco Open Air Culinary Systems **page 74:** courtesy of Allan Block Corp. **page 75:** *top left* courtesy of Outdoor Living Made Easy; *top right* Jay Oliver, Long Island Decking; *bottom left* courtesy of Stout Landscaping Design Build; *bottom right* courtesy of Outdoor Living Made Easy **page 76:** *top* courtesy of Kalamazoo Outdoor Gourmet, designed by Sandy Koepke of Sandy Koepke Interior and Garden Design; *center* courtesy of Outdoor Living Made Easy **page 77:** *top* and *center* courtesy of Danver Stainless Steel Cabinetry; *bottom* courtesy of R. H. Peterson Co. **page 78:** *left* courtesy of Sub-Zero/Wolf; *right* courtesy of Outdoor Living Made Easy **page 79:** *top left* courtesy of Stout Landscaping Design Build; *top right* courtesy of Outdoor Kitchens By Design, Inc., designed by Mark Allen; *center left* courtesy of Danver Stainless Steel Cabinetry; *center right* courtesy of Twin Eagles BBQ Grill; *bottom* courtesy of Sub-Zero/Wolf **page 80:** *top left* courtesy of DCS by Fisher & Paykel Appliances; *top right, bottom left, bottom right* and **page 81:** *all* courtesy of Sur la Table, Inc. **page 82:** courtesy of Outdoor Kitchens By Design, Inc., designed by Mark Allen **page 83:** courtesy of Luxapatio **pages 84–5 and 92:** *all* Clemens Jellema, Fine Decks, Inc. **pages 106–07:** courtesy of Legacy Design-

Build **page 108:** *bottom* courtesy of Majestic Grill Parts **page 109:** *top* Bob Kiefer, Decks by Kiefer; *center* courtesy of Lloyd/Flanders, Inc.; *bottom* courtesy of Stout Landscaping Design Build **page 110:** courtesy of Outdoor Kitchens By Design, Inc., designed by Mark Allen **page 111:** *right* courtesy of Majestic Grill Parts **page 112:** *left* Sergio de Paula, Fogazzo Wood Fired Ovens and Barbecues **page 114:** *center right* Sergio de Paula, Fogazzo Wood Fired Ovens and Barbecues; *bottom right* Dave Toht **page 116:** *all* courtesy of Outdoor Kitchens By Design, Inc., deisigned by Mark Allen **page 128:** Clemens Jellema, Fine Decks, Inc. **page 133:** *bottom right* courtesy of Outdoor Living Made Easy **page 134:** courtesy of Outdoor Kitchens By Design, Inc., designed by Mark Allen **page 139:** *top right* Robin Cox, designed by JMC Designs and built by Collinas Design and Construction **page 150:** courtesy of Danver Stainless Steel Cabinetry **pages 156–59:** *all* courtesy of Allan Block Corp. **page 168:** *bottom right* courtesy of Outdoor Kitchens By Design, Inc., designed by Mark Allen **page 172:** *top* Robin Cox, designed by JMC Designs and built by Collinas Design and Construction; *bottom* courtesy of Majestic Grill Parts **page 173:** *all* courtesy of Stout Landscaping Design Build **page 174:** courtesy of Huettl Landscape Architecture **page 180:** courtesy of Premier Grilling **pages 184–85:** *all* Sergio de Paula, Fogazzo Wood Fired Ovens and Barbecues **pages 186–87:** *all* Clemens Jellema, Fine Decks, Inc. **pages 188–89:** *all* Sergio de Paula, Fogazzo Wood Fired Ovens and Barbecues **page 190:** *bottom left* courtesy of Crimson Valley Landscaping **page 192:** *top right* courtesy of Bull Outdoor Products **page 199:** courtesy of Outdoor Living Made Easy **page 202:** courtesy of Cipriano Landscape Design

Metric Equivalents

Length

1 inch	25.4mm
1 foot	0.3048m
1 yard	0.9144m
1 mile	1.61km

Area

1 square inch	645mm^2
1 square foot	0.0929m^2
1 square yard	0.8361m^2
1 acre	4046.86m^2
1 square mile	2.59km^2

Volume

1 cubic inch	16.3870cm^3
1 cubic foot	0.03m^3
1 cubic yard	0.77m^3

Common Lumber Equivalents

Sizes: Metric cross sections are so close to their U.S. sizes, as noted below, that for most purposes they may be considered equivalents.

Dimensional lumber	1 x 2	19 x 38mm
	1 x 4	19 x 89mm
	2 x 2	38 x 38mm
	2 x 4	38 x 89mm
	2 x 6	38 x 140mm
	2 x 8	38 x 184mm
	2 x 10	38 x 235mm
	2 x 12	38 x 286mm
Sheet sizes	4 x 8 ft.	1200 x 2400mm
	4 x 10 ft.	1200 x 3000mm
Sheet thickness	1/4 in.	6mm
	3/8 in.	9mm
	1/2 in.	12mm
	3/4 in.	19mm
Stud/joist spacing	16 in. o.c.	400mm o.c.
	24 in. o.c.	600mm o.c.

Capacity

1 fluid ounce	29.57mL
1 pint	473.18mL
1 quart	0.95L
1 gallon	3.79L

Weight

1 ounce	28.35g
1 pound	0.45kg

Temperature

Fahrenheit = Celsius x 1.8 + 32
Celsius = Fahrenheit - 32 x 5/9

Nail Size and Length

Penny Size	Nail Length
2d	1"
3d	1 1/4"
4d	1 1/2"
5d	1 3/4"
6d	2"
7d	2 1/4"
8d	2 1/2"
9d	2 3/4"
10d	3"
12d	3 1/4"
16d	3 1/2"

Have a home gardening, decorating, or improvement project?

Look for these and other fine Creative Homeowner books

wherever books are sold

GARDEN SECRETS FOR ATTRACTING BIRDS
Provides information to turn your yard into a mecca for birds.

Over 250 photographs and illustrations.
160 pp.
8½" x 10⅝"
$14.95 (US)
BOOK #: CH274561

CHAR-BROIL'S EVERYBODY GRILLS!
More than 200 recipes for delicious grilled, barbecued, and smoked dishes.

Over 250 photographs.
304 pp.
8½" x 10⅞"
$24.95 (US)
BOOK #: CH253001

CHAR-BROIL'S AMERICA GRILLS!
222 Flavorful recipes that will fire up your appetite.

Over 250 photographs.
304 pp.
8½" x 10⅞"
$24.95 (US)
BOOK #: CH253050

BACKYARD HOMESTEADING
How to turn your yard into a small farm.

Over 235 photographs.
256 pp.
8½" x 10⅞"
$16.95 (US)
BOOK #: CH274800

DECORATING: THE SMART APPROACH TO DESIGN
A go-to how-to guide on decorating, explaining fundamental design principles, for real people.

Over 375 photographs.
288 pp.
8½" x 10⅞"
$21.95 (US)
BOOK #: CH279680

EASY CLOSETS
Introduces homeowners to the variety of closet types and closet systems available.

Over 275 photographs.
160 pp.
8½" x 10⅞"
$14.95 (US)
BOOK #: CH277135

For more information and to order direct, go to **www.creativehomeowner.com**